I0438165

Cherokee Lost

GENE GUTHRIE

iUniverse, Inc.
New York   Bloomington

Cherokee Lost

Copyright © 2009 Gene Guthrie

All rights reserved. No part of this book may be used or reproduced by
any means, graphic, electronic, or mechanical, including photocopying,
recording, taping or by any information storage retrieval system
without the written permission of the publisher except in the case
of brief quotations embodied in critical articles and reviews.

The views expressed in this work are solely those of the author
and do not necessarily reflect the views of the publisher, and the
publisher hereby disclaims any responsibility for them.

iUniverse books may be ordered through booksellers or by contacting:

iUniverse
1663 Liberty Drive
Bloomington, IN 47403
www.iuniverse.com
1-800-Authors (1-800-288-4677)

Because of the dynamic nature of the Internet, any Web addresses or
links contained in this book may have changed since publication and
may no longer be valid. The views expressed in this work are solely those
of the author and do not necessarily reflect the views of the publisher,
and the publisher hereby disclaims any responsibility for them.

ISBN: 978-1-4401-5434-8 (pbk)
ISBN: 978-1-4401-5435-5 (cloth)
ISBN: 978-1-4401-5436-2 (ebk)

Library of Congress Control Number: 2009931976

Printed in the United States of America

iUniverse rev. date: 7/22/2009

In memory of Grandma Ida

Contents

Preface

This story is about my life experiences after I moved in with my grandparents at the age of six and the Cherokee way of living they taught to my brother Jack and me. We lived with our grandfather, Will, for over twelve years before his passing. I learned of his Cherokee heritage from my grandmother.

We were taught how to survive and take care of Mother Earth. We were also taught respect and pride, and, most importantly, how to laugh and enjoy life.

Our Grandpa Will was a boy's grandpa. He endured many hardships along life's journey but never showed bitterness. He fell in love with a pretty mountain girl and stayed faithful to her all his life.

This story can be enjoyed by all ages. It offers many lessons, accompanied by good times.

Although Grandpa Will was removed from his Cherokee people at an early age, he is with his people once more.

Moving In with Grandpa

Sunshine always seemed to twinkle through the shiny new leaves at that time of year. Grandpa said it was because a small breeze was all it took to shake the tender leaves. I took a good deep breath of the air, which smelled of flowering trees and plowed fields.

Mom and Dad had departed after Sunday dinner at Grandpa Will and Grandma Ida's place in Dallas Hollow. Grandpa's place was located about twenty miles north of Chattanooga, Tennessee, at the base of Soddy Mountain, also known as Walden Ridge. My brother Jack and I were both excited about the decision that we would live full-time with our grandparents in early June, 1950. I had finished my first year of grade school.

Grandpa Will was tall, tan, and well-built from all the hard work he'd done, his hands muscular and rough to the touch. His face bore the wrinkles of time. He wore denim overalls with cotton shirts in the summer and flannel in the winter. A colored handkerchief was always hanging from a back pocket of the overalls. He wore a fedora-style hat with a single feather year round. In cooler months, he wore a sport jacket over the overalls. When winter finally came, he added a union suit under his overalls. He walked with a slight limp he had developed from years of carrying heavy loads of ice. He took a walking stick with him now anytime he was outside the house.

Grandpa Will strolled across the yard to a large bench seat located between two hickory trees. As Grandpa sat, he motioned us closer. He took his barlow pocketknife out of one pocket of his overalls and a plug of chewing tobacco from another. He cut off a piece of tobacco and placed it into his cheek. "Now, you two are going to live here with Ida and me. Your mom and dad have bought the hilltop house, and there's no room there for you boys. Why, there's not hardly room enough for one bed, let alone two. It's going to be like all the other times you've been here, except longer.

"You'll have chores to do, but we're going to have fun times too. Like I told you before, if I catch you getting into something that you're not supposed to be into, I'm going to cut your ears off." Grandpa Will always liked to tease us about cutting off our ears. As he reminded us of our responsibilities, I realized he talked of cutting ears off to see Jack squirm on the bench.

About this time, Grandma Ida came out of the house wearing her long garden apron. Holding both bottom edges to make what looked like a basket, she used the apron to gather vegetables. She walked over and said to me, "Why don't we go down to the garden and pick vegetables for supper? Then your grandpa can show you what your daily chores are going to be." Jack stayed with Grandpa on the bench.

As we entered the garden, I asked Grandma Ida if Grandpa was pleased that we were going to live with them, and a large smile came over her wrinkled face.

Grandma started picking green beans and replied, "Now, your grandpa doesn't wear his feelings on his sleeve, but he's the most caring man I've ever been around. It's been over thirty years now, but in the late fall of 1918, terror struck Lookout Mountain. We were all living out on the mountain at the time. My dad and my brother Deck, along with my sister Gracie, died of the flu, as did one of my twin sons, Harl. All of us were really sick then. It left my youngest brother sickly for some time after. I had Carl, the surviving twin, and your Aunt Vernon to care for, and I was pregnant with your mom."

Grandma moved to the tomatoes and continued, "Your grandpa had to build the coffins and get their bodies off Lookout Mountain to Head River Cemetery so they could be buried. A neighbor helped—they took a couple of wagons and teams. They packed picks, shovels, lanterns, blankets, and food for them and the horses. They had to dig the graves because no one else was available, due to all the people dying around Chattanooga and the valleys at the same time. Will said the ice was so bad on the road off the mountain, he loosened some of the horseshoe nails on the team for better traction."

By now we were in the onion patch. Grandma said, "If Will had not stepped up at such a time, my family would have been in deep trouble. Why, all that were left of my mom's kids was one teenage sister, one brother about ten years old, and five brothers and sisters, all younger."

"Who did all the chores after they passed away?" I asked.

"Your grandpa did all the plowing, planting, and livestock care. Timber had to be cut for lumber and firewood. None of my brothers or sisters could have managed the farm without your grandpa. My surviving brothers were so small, it was all they could do to chop kindling, much less tend to the large amounts of firewood needed during the winter. It was six or eight years later before my brothers were big enough to do much plowing. Will was patient; he treated my brothers like they were his sons."

"Has Grandpa always liked boys better?" I asked.

Grandma shrugged. "Will always liked being around boys more than the girls. It must have been a throwback to his Indian youth. He told me his dad brought him and his sisters off the reservation when he was about eight. They took the name Gatlin from the family who raised them. Now, what I've told you will be our secret, so don't tell Jack or your cousins."

When we had finished gathering all the vegetables, Grandma looked over at me and said, "We better get back up to the house now before your grandpa and Jack come looking for us."

My head was abuzz from all the info about Grandpa Will. I couldn't stop smiling. Would Grandpa recognize my smile and suspect Grandma had revealed secrets? I couldn't wait for our next conversation in the garden.

As we arrived back in the yard, Grandma returned to the house. Grandpa took Jack by the hand and motioned me to follow. We first went to the wood pile. "Every day you need to chop enough kindling to fill the box beside the kitchen stove. While you're there, the ash can needs to be emptied. Remember to keep the corn husk box filled—corn husk is what your grandma uses to start the fire."

Next was the corncrib. "Now, you already know how to shell the corn and run the cracker, so keep the bin full and throw a can of feed to the chickens morning and night. Mix about two-thirds corn and a third red sorghum seeds. If you see a brown-colored snake in here, don't get spooked. He's called a bull snake, and I let him alone. He eats mice and will not bother you as long as you give him his space."

From there we went to the chicken house. "Eggs are now yours to collect, afternoons only. If you see corncobs around the nest, leave the eggs. The corncobs are how I'll mark the setting hens' nests; they will hatch the eggs and give us new chicks. And keep the yard and paths swept and raked."

I asked, "Why is it so important to keep them clear? Wouldn't grass be better?"

"If we had grass all over, then the insects, spiders, ticks, mice, and snakes would be in the grass. Your grandma doesn't want to be stepping on any of those. With grass, vermin would be more easily tracked into the house. Besides, you boys don't want to worry about snakes in the grass when you go out to the outhouse, do you?"

The thought of snakes on the path to the outhouse caused both Jack and me to say in unison, "We'll keep it swept clear!"

"I'll take care of the horses, mules, goats, and especially the hogs, for now. The old sow has new piglets, and they're suckling. She's not safe to be around. Why, she'd probably eat one of you if you got in the pen with her. Never get in the pen with the boar; he's even a pill around me. There will be more chores as you get older."

I asked about taking care of Grandma's flower shelves. The shelf unit resembled a picnic bench with a narrow top, and it sat under the tree by the chicken yard. All surfaces held pots of different varieties of flowers. Grandpa said to leave that to Grandma. "Why, I don't even mess with her flowers."

This didn't seem like much for us to do, as we'd already done most of it on our previous visits. I especially appreciated that we wouldn't have to take care of the bees Grandpa kept, and I knew Jack was pleased too. Jack managed to get stung every time he got near the beehives.

As we started back to the house Grandpa said, "Come down to the garden with me." Grandpa stopped at the green onion side and quickly cut off several tops with his pocketknife.

"What's this for?" I asked, puzzled.

Grandpa replied, "I told you we were going to have fun here, so it might as well start at supper."

Before supper, Grandpa washed and cut the onion tops into straws. He placed one in each of our iced tea glasses. "I call them Indian straws," he said, and that was all we had to hear. For several years, using Grandpa's Indian straws became our favorite thing. There was a small amount of onion taste while we used the tops as straws, but what a treat for Jack and me.

After supper Grandpa accompanied us on our chores. He smiled as he gave us advice about how to perform certain tasks more easily. At times Grandpa broke out in laughter watching us try out the new chores. His laughter was contagious. Soon Jack and I were giggling along with Grandpa. It was certainly a learning experience for Jack and me.

One of Grandpa's hunting dogs, Ole Blue, walked along with us. Grandpa told us this was his favorite dog. He told us that after we had been there for a while he was sure Ole Blue would become quite protective of us.

When the chores were done, we all sat on the bench. Ole Blue curled up at Grandpa's feet, slightly under the bench. Maggie, one of Blue's littermates, curled up at our feet, while the rest of the dogs rested behind the bench, giving Ole Blue and Maggie their space. Grandpa whittled on a piece of wood as he told us stories. Some were about his chores and adventures as a youth, while others were about hunting or fishing. I could have spent the night listening to Grandpa talk.

Grandpa looked toward the house and said, "We better head inside. Your grandma has your baths ready. Besides, there're going to be a lot of evenings on this ol' bench yet to come."

As we walked to the house, I suddenly realized I was going to have more one-on-one time with Grandpa Will than ever before. I would not have to share our time with my parents or my cousins. Other visits had been taken up with eating and play, allowing very little time to be alone with Grandpa or Grandma. I knew this was a life-changing experience, and I was ready to enjoy it to its fullest.

When we got into the house Grandma said, "I've got your baths ready. When you finish, we can listen to a little radio before bed."

Baths were taken in the large galvanized washtub in the kitchen by the wood cookstove. Grandma would place a few kitchen chairs around the tub, hanging towels over the chair backs to provide us with privacy. It also created a barrier to keep the heat from the stove in the bath area. She heated water on the wood cookstove and mixed the water until the temperature was perfect for bathing. She was a stickler for washing the parts boys usually skip, like behind the ears.

After our baths were completed and we had put on our pajamas, we settled in the living room. Grandpa turned on the radio and sat beside me in one of the two rockers. Jack curled up in Grandma's lap. Grandma had brewed hot chocolate for each of us. Flickering shadows filled the room from the glow of two coal oil lamps. All of the windows were open, and we heard thumping sounds when bugs, drawn to the light, hit the screens. The air outside was still but alive with the sounds of country life. Grandma's ol' cat was curled up beside the chair where she sat.

As we sat there Grandma told me she was glad Mom and Dad had bought the hilltop house, but even more, she was happy we would be living with them full-time. She reminded us of the importance of doing what we were told. She said things were going to be different here with her and Grandpa Will. She told us Grandpa did not believe in striking children as a punishment. She said our mom's temper seemed to get the best of her at times. We were told the Indian in Grandpa did not allow for beating his livestock, much less children.

The image of our first night has remained a snapshot in my mind.

The trips to and from the outhouse were a learning experience. The first year we were there, trips after dark were made using a flashlight Dad had given us. We used the flashlight sparingly, as batteries were expensive. Grandpa told us how when he was our age, he'd used a candle placed inside a metal container with holes. He said the carrying container allowed light to shine and kept the candle from being blown out by the wind. We still were uneasy about what might be along the path or inside the outhouse. Ole Blue wasn't much for following us to the outhouse, but Maggie always kept an eye on us. It seemed she was determined to be with us two boys any time she spotted an opening. In what seemed like no time, Jack, me, and the two dogs were inseparable. Grandpa didn't mind sharing his dogs. He said all boys need dogs.

Grandma kept herbs planted along the path; most gave off aromas when brushed against, especially the mint. There was even a row of honeysuckle along the chicken-yard-fence side of the path. During the warmer months, hummingbirds and butterflies could be seen feeding on honeysuckle. In winter months, Grandma covered the herbs with straw to ward off freezing.

I remember asking Grandpa why Grandma's clothesline had long poles, which she used sometimes. He told me the poles were for when she had large items like sheets or his overalls to hang out. The poles would keep the items from dragging on the ground.

Grandpa showed us how he trimmed the wicks for the coal oil lamps. Grandpa said, "Now, some people added water to the oil basins during the Great Depression because the wicks were short, and they didn't have enough coal oil to fill the basins."

I asked what the water did. He explained the kerosene, or coal oil, as he called it, would float to the top, enabling the short wick to reach the coal oil. He proudly stated, "My dad told me our people had knowledge of tar and oil many years before the settlers came. He said it could be found in seeps all along the mountains. Why, they even used the tar to make night torches." I still have visions of Grandpa's people walking after dark, using small poles dipped in tar to make night torches.

Summer

The first summer brought many new experiences. Berry picking and preserve making were really a little scary. It was common for our aunts and cousins to berry pick with us. First came the berry patches and several encounters with black snakes. Maggie was eager to dispatch any snakes. Maggie's sudden barking and charging as startling as the sight of the snake. We each carried one or two buckets for berries. Grandma had us wear long sleeve shirts to keep the berry briars from scratching our arms. The blackberry canes were the worst. The curved thorns really cut when we reached into the canes to the riper berries. It was common to come back home with over five gallons of berries.

When we got back home Grandpa would check us for ticks. Most of the time he would find one or two and quickly dispose of them. Chigger bites were treated by rinsing our feet and legs in one of the washtubs' solution of water and chlorine bleach.

After berry picking came the worst of all chores: "Go crawl under the house and bring out all the jars you can find," I heard Grandpa say the first day of berry picking. All I could think of was the possibility of running into a snake under the house. But after lots of reassurance from both Grandpa and Grandma, I managed to overcome my fears and retrieve all the canning jars without breaking any. Any jars that had deep chips or cracks around the threaded tops were taken to the barn and stored for uses that didn't require a perfect seal. The jars not used for berries were later used for vegetables.

Later in the day I helped Grandma boil the jars. This was accomplished by first washing the jars in soapy water and then dipping each jar into boiling water. The jars were placed on clean dish towels.

Grandma washed and cleaned the berries we had picked. The berries were cooked with coarse sugar. Grandma kept us back when she filled the jars. She said it was because the sugar would make a nasty burn if any were to splatter onto us. We watched as she filled the jars with cooked berries. The canned whole berries would later be used in cobbler pies.

The jams and jellies were poured into drinking glasses and sealed with paraffin, which had been melted in an old pan on the stove. The preserves were poured into pint-size canning jars. The preserves and whole berries were placed in a cool bath after the tops were in place. Grandma said this created a better seal.

Berry picking happened every two or three days during berry season. Some days it was blackberries, other days dewberries or wild strawberries.

When the peaches were ready, we would all go down to the orchard and pick peaches in the morning. Grandma would clean and cut up most of them. She canned several quarts of sliced peaches for cobbler pies. A few of the peaches were dipped first in boiling water and then into cool water so the skin was easily removed. These were packed along with cloves. Grandma called them pickled peaches.

Grandma Ida seemed to enjoy having us help her with the canning. She said it was nice having kids back in the kitchen. I must have surely bored her with all my questions during the first summer, although she never showed anything but a smile.

The rewards of helping Grandma Ida prepare the preserves and jellies were delightful: not only did we share the experience and learn how they were made, but after the pots were emptied Jack and I were each given biscuits to dip into the fruit that remained. Thoughts of warm, fresh preserves remain a fond memory.

Grandpa Will received a bowl of warm preserves, along with biscuits. The treat brought quite the smile, and I realized Grandma Ida had served this up to Grandpa Will often over the years.

Grandma always used the quart-size jars for vegetable canning. The vegetables were placed in the jars, and the lids were applied. Then they were cooked in a deep hot water canning pot. She canned enough vegetables and fruits to fill one shelved wall in the corn crib. She kept a shelf in the kitchen stocked with jars. When she'd use food from the kitchen supply, she'd restock from the corn crib. Jack or I would do the retrieving after Grandma told us what she needed.

One day in late summer, Grandma came out of the house and hollered for Grandpa and us to come quick. She pointed to a short, fat snake under her dresser. "Take it out and get rid of it. My old cat's got to be watched. Now, if you boys see her trying to get in, you've got to check her mouth. Cats bring their captures home for show. It's important to check. This old puff adder isn't any harm, but a copperhead or rattler would be."

We took the snake outside, and Grandpa showed us how the puff adder spit when approached. He pointed out the upturned snout and told us the puff adder dug for grubs using its nose. We took the snake out into the woods and released it. Grandpa said, "If the critter eats grubs, it's a friend of mine."

I had my first experience of churchgoing during that summer. Grandma went to a church down by the cemetery. She took Jack and me with her and encouraged our participation in Sunday school, vacation Bible school, and choir as we grew older.

The church went under the Baptist name but was really one step away from snake handling. It was common for people to start shouting and speaking in tongues. On occasion, some would walk on top of the pews. A few years later, my sister reported it had traumatized her, and she had a hard time going to church as an adult.

Grandpa didn't attend, but I can still remember what he said one day. "The church down there isn't going to save you; it's what you do when you're not at the church that will."

When I asked what he'd meant by his previous statement, he replied, "Now, I'm not saying anything bad about the preacher there. But I've seen plenty of folks from the church and others drinking and carousing around during the week. I respect your grandma for her beliefs, but me, I live every day as if it were my last, with no time to ask for forgiveness. A lot of mistletoe and dogwood people attend your grandma's church."

I asked what mistletoe and dogwood people were. Grandpa explained that some only attended church at Christmas or Easter.

Grandma always wore a dark dress with a crocheted white collar to church. She took along black shoes with a raised heel, but she wore her slippers on the walk to church and changed after she arrived. She carried a Bible, along with a hand fan on summer days.

I remember asking Grandpa why she didn't walk to church in her dress shoes. He said her feet were too flat and wide from going barefoot so much, and her feet hurt when she wore the dress shoes.

After church on Sundays, Grandpa Will and Grandma Ida's place was where most of the relatives living in Dallas Hollow could be found. Sometimes the preacher and his family would also be there. It was a sure bet country-fried chicken and fresh vegetables would be served. Grandma usually made several pies or cakes for dessert.

We ate simple country food at most meals. Grandpa seemed to enjoy the foods of his people the most: sweet potatoes, squash, pumpkin, corn cooked any style, pork, fish, and all forms of wild game. He loved the wild berries, especially wild strawberries, and fruits like persimmon. He also liked wild grapes, such as the muscadine and possum grapes. As for nuts from the native trees, chestnuts were his favorite.

Grandpa said when he was our age that chestnuts had been quite abundant. He told us a lot of families had lived on the nuts when times were bad. Once he said he had broken the chestnut out of its spiny shell with his bare feet. This didn't surprise me, as my feet had become pretty callused from going barefooted. He ate hickory nuts on a regular basis. I thought they were too difficult to open and only yielded a small amount of edible nut.

Grandpa liked what he called Johnny cakes, or fried corn bread patties. I later learned the Confederate soldiers ate the cakes out of necessity, hence the name Johnny cakes. Even though Grandma didn't like fried cakes, there were always some on the table. I think she would have cooked most anything if it were something Grandpa wanted.

Grandpa talked about cooking a small goat in a pit, but he never cooked one in such a way while we were with him. I suppose it was a memory from his youth. I have often wondered if Grandpa had memories of pit cooking with his father.

Grandma enjoyed fixing a hearty breakfast. Biscuits were a staple, along with eggs. Grandpa preferred the stronger tasting eggs like duck or sometimes a double yoke egg. Sausage or salt back was the usual meat. Grits were served in the cooler months.

Grandma was the perfect example of a country cook. She enjoyed cooking and was pleased watching as our young palates learned new tastes. She certainly seemed to come up with many new things for Jack and me to try. Preparing the foods was a treat for her, but explaining how she learned of them gave her even more pleasure. All we had to do was ask questions about food and Grandma would beam a large smile.

The round oak table had several items in the center all the time: salt, pepper, bottled peppers with vinegar, sorghum, honey, preserves, and chowchow. In season were fresh hot peppers, radishes, and green onions, which were placed into a canning jar with water. Sugar was not offered, as most everything was presweetened, like sweet tea.

Grandpa showed Jack and me how to crop chicken wings the first summer we were there. He used an old pair of scissors and cut the long flight feathers off one wing. He said this way they couldn't fly over the fence and get eaten by the dogs. Jack and I caught the chickens while Grandpa trimmed. To Jack and me this was quite a task. Grandma kept Rhode Island Red chickens, which get quite large. Catching one was only part of the task. Holding onto a flapping chicken at our ages tested our wills. The roosters were the worst; they had long spurs and were very willing to use them in defense. A few times Grandpa had to step in when an ol' rooster got mad.

There were a few bantam hens and roosters, and Grandpa didn't crop their wings. These worked the garden area and were quite mean, as chickens go. Even the dogs left them alone. Ole Blue ran most of the critters, with the exception of the bantams. Grandpa told of Blue's first and only encounter with the bantams. He said it only lasted a minute or so. After the bantam got onto Blue's head, he decided it was best to leave those roosters alone. He said a few months later little Maggie decided she was going to put the bantam roosters in their place. After she got her smacking, Grandpa swears he saw Blue wearing a large smile.

One summer day Jack was sitting on the front edge of the porch. Two ol' bantam roosters got into a fight and chased each other all over the yard. They ended up in Jack's lap. What a sight! Jack was trying to get up, with the two roosters still going at each other. Somehow Jack managed to get out from between the two fighting roosters without getting hurt himself.

The front porch hosted another painful event for Jack. He was sitting on the front edge eating a peanut butter and jelly sandwich. A couple of yellow jackets lit on the sandwich. Jack took another bite and wound up with two very unhappy yellow jackets in his mouth. Yellow jackets are quite different than bees. They can sting repeatedly. Needless to say, Jack took quite a stinging. Grandpa had a very caring talk with Jack afterward, telling him he had to be very careful while eating outside.

I remember asking Grandpa about the feathers he and his people wore. He said they were badges of courage earned by the Cherokee boys and men. They were usually of the hawk or eagle variety. When I asked how he had earned the feather he wore in his hat, he said Grandma had given him the feather not long after their first children were born. I never asked what he'd done to earn it, as I remembered the conversation with Grandma about the aftermath of the flu on the mountain.

The second summer we were there the rural power company extended power lines into Dallas Hollow. The house was wired with one light bulb in the center of each room. A screw-in receptacle was placed in each light socket so extension cords could be plugged in. Dad brought Grandma Ida a ringer washer and refrigerator. Mom found several pairs of metal pant stretchers and gave them to Grandma. Grandma used the pant stretchers when drying Levi's jeans or Grandpa's overalls. She liked using them because the fabric dried flat, with creases.

The washing machine was placed outside on a side porch, and a light receptacle with a pull cord was installed to power the washer. The new electrical item Jack and I most liked was the porch light. Now we could see down the path to the outhouse. The light also extended our playtime. Having power allowed another first, a large console radio, which could be played forever without needing batteries. Before power, the old hand-crank record player, along with a small battery-powered radio, had been the entertainment.

Most evenings were filled with voices coming from the radio. Grandma would usually knit or crochet while Grandpa, Jack, and I played regular or Chinese checkers. We listened to *The Green Hornet, Amos and Andy, Kids Say the Darnedest Things,* and *Jack Benny.* Grandpa enjoyed Art Linkletter's program *Kids Say the Darnedest Things* best. He enjoyed anything related to children.

I saw my first butter substitute during that summer. It was called oleo and came in a soft, clear package. In the center of the package was a small red ball. After some squeezing, the red ball burst and, once mixed in, it turned the oleo yellow.

One late summer afternoon a thunderstorm rumbled through Dallas Hollow. Clouds were dark and low. The thunder rose from a soft rumble to a fierce drumming. Distant crackles of lightning suddenly became loud clashes, lighting up the entire inside of the house. It was completely dark outside except when the lightning struck.

Grandpa said, "This one's going to be a doozy!"

About the same time, a bolt of lightning struck the front post of the chicken yard. We looked out and saw the post in splinters and part of the fence down. Some of the chickens were starting to exit the pen. Grandpa motioned for us to follow him. When we got there, we noticed several chickens had been struck. It looked like someone had set them on fire—they lay, smoking, on the ground.

We fixed the fence and gathered the loose chickens. Grandpa told us to feed the burnt chickens to the hogs. We asked why we couldn't eat them. He explained, "The innards are cooked into the meat. You can't eat them now."

Grandma came out to check on the repair of the fence. It was still sprinkling rain, and then the sun broke through the clouds. Thunder still sounded in the distance. Grandma smiled and stated, "Boys, when it rains and the sun shines together, the devil is beating his wife."

That lightning strike had been an act of God, but another incident involving burning chickens happened a few years later.

The house next door to Mom and Dad's hilltop house had been purchased by a retired pharmacist from Chicago. Why he decided to move to Dallas Hollow always puzzled our whole family. He planted a garden and hired Jack and me for various jobs around the house and garden. He raised chickens and gave them shots of vitamins and antibiotics. One day he discovered one of the chickens was sick. He proceeded to ensure it would not infect the others. He struck the chicken with a small board and poured gasoline over it.

He lit a match, and then the chicken jumped up, completely in flames, and ran under his house. As the flaming chicken ran past, it made a loud swooshing sound. Jack later said it sounded like a jet engine. I quickly took a rake and removed the bird before the house caught fire too. Later Grandpa said, "If you hadn't been there, the ol' man would've burned no telling how many of us out. Now, you boys be careful around him. He's as crazy as a Betsy Bug."

Jack and I worked for the ol' man for several more years. Some jobs were strange, like when we picked all the rocks larger than a marble from the garden. Grandpa said that was a continuing process, as the rain only exposed more rocks. The neighbor paid well, and that meant good spending money for us. Grandpa said that if we didn't take advantage of the opportunity, then someone else would.

My cousin from my dad's side came to visit one summer. He was from the Chicago area, and Dad thought it would be good for him to experience country life. Well, let me tell you, Jack and I had quite the time teasing him. He was raised in a large city and had never seen fresh garden foods.

I took advantage of his innocence shortly after he arrived. The three of us boys sat down for dinner. Grandma always ate hot chile peppers from her garden. There was a small bowl in the center of the table with several fresh peppers inside. I spotted one pepper; Grandma had bitten half off and placed the remainder back into the bowl. These particular peppers were so hot Grandma hardly ever ate more than a half.

While Grandma was fixing our sandwiches, I retrieved the half-eaten pepper and moved it close to my mouth, pretending I was chewing it. My cousin looked over and asked what I was eating. I quickly said, "They're sweet peppers, and we eat them like candy down here."

He took the bait, selected a whole pepper, placed it in his mouth, and began to chew. Well, let me tell you, Dallas Hollow never heard a scream like was let out of that boy's mouth. Grandma asked what had happened. Jack and I both said in unison, "He wanted to try one of your peppers, and I guess he couldn't handle it."

It took quite some time for the burning to stop. Grandma gave him butter and honey, which always worked.

When we went outside afterward, Grandpa winked and said, "Now you boys take better care of your cousin. He'll need your help while staying here." I knew he was trying to give us a scolding for what we had done, but his kidding side was pleased. Jack and I still teased our cousin during his summer visit but never to the extent of the hot peppers. Grandpa seemed pleased by the fact we did teach him a lot about rural life.

As Jack and I grew older and explored more of the surrounding area, we became aware of the Klan members. Some evenings they would form a caravan of autos. Each auto had one or two Klan members inside. They would usually travel with the dome lights turned on. Grandpa said it was so you would notice them. He also said it was kind of useless. "When you see a lot of autos with men wearing sheets, it's pretty evident who they are."

He told Jack and me it was okay for us to go down by the forks in the road to watch them burn the crosses. I still remember what he said: "Now, you can watch, but you boys be careful not to get mixed up with them.

Don't dislike people by their color but by their actions. Why, it's most of them in the sheets who really need to be strung up."

Jack and I, along with several of the boys from Dallas Hollow, would usually slip down to the forks to watch each time the Klan burned the crosses. We were always careful to stay in the shadows. I remembered what Grandpa had said about not getting mixed up with them.

I was tempted once to sabotage their autos but decided it might bring retaliation from the members. I had thought about stuffing potatoes up the tailpipes of the cars with a broomstick handle. It would have prevented the cars from starting. I thought it would have been funny watching them in daylight trying to retrieve their cars. I told Grandpa what I'd thought of, and he laughed as much as I'd seen him. He said it would have been a good one but agreed it was best not to have done it.

One morning Grandpa took us down to the barn's side shed, where we'd been emptying the stove ash into the rock-lined pit.

"What are we going to do?" I asked eagerly.

"Make lye," he replied with a smile.

"But, Grandpa, you said never to lie!"

Grandpa broke into laughter and replied, "It's not whoppers we're going to tell. We're going to make lye for your grandma's soap."

Grandpa took a wooden hopper about three feet tall out of the shed and placed it on top of four large rocks.

It was tapered, larger at the top. He motioned us to look inside. The bottom was covered by a layer of small rocks. "Go get some straw, and cover the rocks 'til it's as deep as your hands." It looked like a nesting box, but not for long. Grandpa suddenly started filling the box almost to the top with ash from the pit. He placed a wooden bucket under the small hole at the bottom of the hopper. He poured three buckets of water from the rain barrel over the ashes.

Grandpa started a fire under a large iron cooking kettle and emptied the yellowish water that had drained from the hopper into the kettle.

"Now go get me one egg and several chicken feathers from the hen house."

I was definitely confused by now.

When I returned, Grandpa was stirring the kettle with a large wooden paddle. Grandma stood several feet away, holding Jack's hand. As the mixture cooked down to a thick-looking paste, Grandpa dropped the egg in. At first it sank, then soon it bobbed to the top. Within a short time the egg was floating on top of the mixture.

"Well, the lye's ready. Hand me the feather, and I'll show you the other way to tell." Grandpa dipped the feather into the mix, and it quickly started to dissolve. "When the ash water eats the feather, then it's lye."

Grandma came over now and took the wooden paddle.

Grandpa took me over to where Jack was watching. Grandpa was smiling as Grandma started putting in chunks of lard.

"What's she doing?" I asked.

His smile seemed to get larger as he replied, "Making soap."

Soon she poured the thick mixture into a wooden tray. Moments before it hardened, she cut it into bars.

"Now, this is the soap your grandma uses. When the bars get small, she uses them to scrub the floors. It bleaches the wood to a lighter color, making it look cleaner. You can also see anything on the floors easier when they're bleached."

I asked, "Is lye what we put down the outhouse to keep it from smelling?"

Grandpa chuckled and said, "No, it's not lye we use. The powder we use is called lime. I get it from the gristmill where I take the corn. Now, as soon as we clean up the kettle and store the hopper, we'll go looking for more wild strawberries."

This was all Jack and I needed to hear. We knew it predestined another stroll through the woods with Grandpa. Each time we traveled through the woods, Grandpa would point out different birds and their songs. Once he pointed out a mocking bird and commented, "Now, there's the ol' trickster. He's so good at copying other birds the Great Spirit has marked his wings with white stripes so you'd know it was him and not the other birds singing."

Grandpa somehow had learned about all the plants and animals in the woods. It surely was his people's way. He had knowledge of all the night sounds. Dallas Hollow was alive with bird and insect calls at night. The tree frogs and crickets were always in the foreground of the sounds. Intermixed were screech and hoot owl calls, the katydid, and the whip-poor-will. Grandpa said the whip-poor-will knew his name.

We would set on the bench after dark, and Grandpa would point out different sounds while we guessed at what made them. He said as soon as we could master the sounds and how the sound makers lived, then we could safely walk the area at night.

We learned only the uncommon sounds that were to be noticed for our safety: the panther, bear, stray dog, or—worse—a man. Grandpa's idea was great because all we had to worry about after dark in the woods was where we were stepping. This way we didn't trip or, worse, get snake-bitten.

I remember him showing Jack and me the star constellation called the Big Dipper. He said you could tell what time of year it was by how the Dipper was positioned in the sky. In the summer months, the Dipper spills its water, and in the winter months, it holds the water. He also knew the polar star could be found by sighting along the front edge of the Dipper. He told us any time we were going somewhere at night to remember which direction we were traveling in relation to the polar star and we could always find our way back. He also pointed out the moon and its east-to-west travels.

Even though I am older now and have performed a lot of night flights in my own aircraft, I still catch myself looking up to the Dipper and polar star before departing. It's a reassurance that brings the warm feeling of remembering Grandpa. Sometimes I think of him when things become hurried in life and realize I need to slow down and savor the moment.

Grandpa liked showing us all the edible fruits, berries, and nuts—especially the things his people would have eaten. He said if you knew what was edible and knew how to locate the right plants and trees, you would never starve. Later in the summer, we discovered Grandpa's favorite grape, the muscadine. The grape was about the diameter of a quarter, with a tough skin and a musky flavor that was definitely an acquired taste. When you knew where to look in the woods, it was like mushrooms—they were all over the place. He showed us a plant called the mayapple. It grew low and had a single stem about a foot and half tall. Its leaves were large, and a dark green fruit hid under the leaves. Grandpa said the fruit was edible but tasted bland. He said his people used the roots along with sassafras for treatments. He showed us several kinds of tree bark and sagelike plants that were used for different treatments.

One such sage plant Grandpa called rabbit tobacco. He said it was called rabbit tobacco because of the way it grew. The stem grew about one and a half foot tall before it forked and produced blooms. The single leaves attached to the stem between the ground level, and the forks were smoked. Grandpa said it was the right height for rabbits and little boys.

Grandpa said young boys of his people usually started smoking with this plant. Of course when Jack and I heard this, we wanted to give it a try. We both switched to regular smoking tobacco as soon as possible. I learned later the Western Indians use two-toed sage in smoke purification ceremonies. I don't think Jack or I either one purified our lungs by smoking rabbit tobacco. We didn't always copy what Grandpa did. Neither of us ever chewed tobacco as adults.

At supper one day, Grandma said, "Will, I saw a chicken hawk in the big oak tree by the chicken yard while you were gone with the boys."

Grandpa explained to us that the chicken hawk would eat all of the young chickens if given the chance. So any time we saw a hawk in the trees, we should shoot at it with our slingshots.

Later during the summer we managed to sight several hawks and scattered them with our new shooters. We had discovered by then that hard green crab apples made great ammunition for our slingshots. Our keeping the hawks at bay seemed to give much pleasure to Grandma.

One afternoon Grandpa came up from the woods exclaiming, "Get Grandma and tell her the bees have swarmed! Bring the old pots from the barn and ya'll follow me."

When we got to the woods Grandpa told us to start banging on the pots. After awhile he stopped under a large pine tree and said, "They've swarmed around the queen there on the limb."

As I looked up I spotted a large ball of bees surrounding part of a limb.

Grandpa took a handsaw and his bee smoker up

the ladder that he had retrieved from the barn. After delivering several puffs of smoke, he sawed the limb off, being careful not to let it drop. He carried the limb back to the beehives and scraped the bees off into a new hive.

I asked, "Why didn't the bees try to sting you or leave the limb?"

Grandpa explained the bees had only one thing on their minds. They were committed to surrounding the young queen, and she was in the middle of the ball of bees on the limb. When he scraped her into the hive, they followed. He explained the fact that a hive could only have one queen. He told Jack and me if we ever saw a swarm of bees come out of one of the hives, we were to follow them while banging on the pots. He said the loud noise would make the bees land in the nearest tree.

In late summer, Grandpa gathered the season's honey. He covered his head with a bee bonnet. It had what looked like screen wire all the way around. He put on long gloves and fired up the bee smoker. Grandpa said the smoke disoriented the bees and calmed them.

He opened the top of each hive and removed the vertical comb hangers. Upon finding a comb hanger completely filled with honey, he placed it into a large metal dish pan. The hangers that were less than half full of honey were not removed. Grandpa left these for the bees' nourishment and survival. He kept smoking the bees until most had left the dish pan.

After he had removed all the comb hangers and the bees had returned to the hive, he took the honey-laden dish pan to the kitchen. He gently scraped both sides of the comb, exposing the honey. He propped the comb upright and allowed the honey to drain into the pan.

The honey then was placed into quart canning jars. The wax comb was rolled into balls. Grandma kept some to rub on her lips. She said it kept them from cracking in the cold weather. Grandpa used it on saws and other tools. They said the bee's wax was a useful lubricant and even eased the cutting of wood.

I asked why we didn't wait to harvest until later in the year, as surely the bees would have produced more honey by then. Grandpa said, "We have to leave enough for the bees. We want to make sure they survive the winter. Besides, the honey flows from the comb easier in warm weather."

Another day, Grandpa had Jack and me clean the old salt from the saltbox in the corn crib. He said to spread it around the edge of the house.

I asked why, and Grandpa replied, "The salt will keep grass from growing, and slugs and insects don't seem to like it."

After the salt box had been cleaned, Grandpa poured several sacks of new salt into the box. When the salt was six inches deep, it was smoothed by hand and covered again.

"It's ready for another winter now," Grandpa said.

I asked Grandpa if we should sprinkle some of the salt around Grandma's herbs in order to help keep the grass away.

This brought quite a chuckle, "Go over to your

grandma and ask how she keeps grass out of the herbs."
I knew he was trying to show me something, so I strolled
over to where Grandma was watering her flowers.

I asked her how she kept grass out of the herbs.

She replied, "Well, I use the old coffee grounds and
work them into the soil around the herbs. It helps keep
the soil moist but stops the weeds along with the bugs.
I do the same with my flowers except I use the old tea
leaves. In all except the cactus plants, I sprinkle the
leaves right in the pots. Now, your grandpa thinks it
makes the flowers bloom prettier, but it really only holds
the moisture."

Summer was filled with the harvesting of vegetables
and canning. I kept the jars supplied and helped Grandma
whenever necessary. There was always a lot of vegetable
picking, prep work, and cleaning. Green beans and okra
took the longest. Sometimes I could not imagine we
could ever eat all the things Grandma had canned. But
by late spring when the stored supply began to empty, it
would become clear Grandma had usually canned the
correct amount. Since she witnessed her parents and
grandparents can foods prior to having her own family
with Grandpa, I realized she could tell by the number
of mouths to feed what needed to be stored.

On one of the trips to the garden to harvest vegetables
for canning, I asked why she and Grandpa left Lookout
Mountain.

She said after her brothers were almost grown,
Grandpa Will came to her one night and said, "You'd
better start packing. We're moving to town."

"I knew there must have been a misunderstanding between my mom and your grandpa. Your grandpa had been a blacksmith out on the mountain. Remember the shop on the left side of the driveway at Mom's? Well, in there was where your grandpa set up his blacksmith shop.

"Now, some of your trifling cousins will probably say the shop was my dad's, but the proof of the pudding was where it was built. If it had been my dad's, it would have been attached to the barn. Why, the barn was where all the livestock and plows were kept. You don't think my dad would have carried the plows all the way from the barn to the road for fixing, do you? The old shed still has Will's anvil and forge, along with some of his tools, in it.

"People came from all over the mountain to have him fix wagon wheels or plows or to shoe their horses. I can remember hearing people say they were coming out to Will's place to get something made or fixed. Anyway, I never questioned him.

"We moved to Eastlake, and he started working the coal delivery business. He left most of the blacksmith tools and a lot of the farm equipment when we moved. He never was a blacksmith for hire after we left Lookout Mountain."

I asked Grandma what had happened to the coal business, and she said, "The Depression came along, and people couldn't afford the coal."

Again I asked, "What did Grandpa do then?"

Grandma smiled and said, "Well, your grandpa

was always ready for about anything that came up. He decided the ice delivery business would be good because people needed it to keep their butter and milk from spoiling. He said he would use the wagons and team from the coal works. And so with what seemed like little effort, he was delivering ice. He delivered coal in the winter, but the ice delivery was year round. Although in the winter months, ice was in less demand. This was always okay with me; I liked the fact he wasn't climbing stairs in the winter carrying ice blocks on his back. He ran the business until we moved out here a couple of years back."

Later, when we were out on the mountain for a reunion during summer, I looked in the shed, and sure enough, all the blacksmith tools were still there. I never told Grandpa I had talked to Grandma about his time on Lookout Mountain.

Sometime later, I did tell Grandpa my mom had said he had been a blacksmith, and I asked, "Why'd you quit blacksmithing?" He smiled, then shrugged his shoulders and said, "Oh, it was too hard work."

I knew nothing could have been too hard for him, so I never mentioned the conversation Grandma and I had in the garden.

I changed the subject to his coal business. "Mom said you delivered coal and used the mules." He smiled and said, "Yeah, back then others were doing it, but they were all starting to use trucks. Since coal was very light, I stuck to using the wagon. I could get it around people's yards without making ruts or breaking anything. I could get my mules to go anywhere I asked. I even built wood chutes so I could dump the coal under customers' houses, as most had basements with coal bins."

One day when I was about fourteen and had hunted out on Lookout Mountain with my dad, I went to the garden with Grandma to pick vegetables. I had always honored Grandma's wishes about our private conversations and kept our conversations to myself. Later I would realize she had confided more to me than to my mom. I think it had become a blessing to have someone she could share things with.

I asked, "Why doesn't Grandpa like going out on Lookout Mountain?" Grandma looked my way. After what seemed like eternity, she replied, "I guess you should know the reason. I know you are the age to know more. What I'm about to say is to be treated like what I told you about your grandpa when you and Jack moved in with Will and me. Don't say anything to your cousins or anyone else about what I'm going to say.

"Remember the part about Will and me leaving the mountain? Well, that was when your mom was about eight years old. We had all been living at the house there on the mountain. Will and I had moved into Mom's house after the flu had killed Dad, my brother and sister, and one of my twin sons.

"Mom and the girls were in one room, the boys in another, and Will and I had one to ourselves. It's never calm with two families in a household.

"We had all worked hard keeping things going after

my dad passed away, but none of us as hard as Will. I remember Will working all day in his shop there by the road and then tending to livestock and crops half of the night.

"Your grandpa mentioned he was going to add on to the house so as to give more sleeping rooms for the kids. Well, my mom flew off the handle and told Will he wasn't going to do anything else around there without permission. She stated the place was not his. She said she was tired of hearing the place referred to as Will's place.

"Your grandpa said the thing that hurt him the most was when she said the farm was going to my boys and surely not to some Indian like him. Those words seemed like an arrow in his heart. He said my mom had the temper and was mean, like most of her family. He said some of my brothers and sisters even had Mom's prejudice in them. Will would often say he could tell which of us was from my dad's side and who was from my mom's.

"At this time, my younger brothers were about seventeen and nineteen years old. Will told me they could keep the place, and he wouldn't be surprised if the oldest of the two hadn't egged my mom on. He said my brother had my mom's temper. My brother stayed on the place, and it cost him the chance to marry. As time went on, the farm would not support a family.

"Will said he didn't mind leaving his shop equipment there because neither one of the boys could use it. He always said none of them knew anything about working teams, and I reckon he was right, because soon after we left they bought a tractor.

"Why, I've even heard some of my kin say Will and I left the mountain so Will could grow cotton. When we left the mountain, boll weevils had infested the cotton around here for almost ten years. All the cotton crops had failed, and even the shipping had all but stopped by then.

"We had no insecticides during those times, so within a few years of the arrival of the critters most everyone had abandoned growing cotton. Besides, where do you think Will and I would have got the money to buy a farm and equipment? The banks had quit lending money, if they were still in business. A lot of the banks had closed doors by then.

"Will took good care of us during the Depression by working the coal business and raising a large garden there at Eastlake. Believe me, life would have been a lot easier for us on the mountain during the Depression.

"Anyway, Will has not had anything much to do with the brother who was still there running the farm. Why, my brother was still mad at me because I moved with your grandpa. You know, I guess they never stopped to think maybe the place should have gone to the oldest of the surviving kids, which would have been me. My ol' Cherokee would have taken care of us there on the mountain. He had stepped in and saved us after my dad passed away.

"My brother told me once that not me or any of my little half breeds would ever have any part of the mountain place. You know, I wouldn't trade your grandpa for a hundred of my brothers. I was always proud to have children with Cherokee bloodlines. I see your grandpa's calm attitude and outlook in several of my grandchildren. At times when I watch you and Jack, I think this must have been what Will was like at your age. After all that has happened, your grandpa was always cordial around my brother or my mom. I'll take my ol' Indian over anyone else I've laid eyes on.

"Now, your uncle Carl took it harder than your grandpa. He had spent the first several years of his life there on the mountain. He was so hurt he moved away to Florida before the War. As soon as he finished school, he was out of here like a scalded dog. When he does come home, it's only us or his sisters he visits."

After my conversation with Grandma, it became difficult to be at the mountain place. I usually went out to the orchard or revisited the old shop by the road. Each time I went into the shop, I noticed the dust and rust, more evident than the last visit, and understood my grandpa had been correct. None of the boys were ever able to make use of his anvil and forge.

I recalled an earlier conversation with Grandma when she had referred to disappointments Grandpa had endured. I knew now he had witnessed the hurt his own children had gone through when he and Grandma moved off Lookout Mountain. I had known my own mother seemed to carry a lot of bitterness, but I also remembered Grandpa saying she had a lot of my great-grandmother in her. Mom's sister outwardly seemed to have handled it better, or maybe she moved on to find happiness in her own family. Mom's brother had married but had no children. Could it be somehow he had not moved on and was still carrying a grudge for the Krogers?

Visiting the shop would always bring me a smile. I knew none of my cousins had ever thought of why the shop was built by the road. I would recall Grandpa leaving the equipment there to remind Grandma's brothers how little they really knew.

Grandpa shared so much of his blacksmith knowledge with Jack and me. He didn't have his large forge or anvils. The work was performed on a small combination forge and grinding wheel. The forge part was about the size of a charcoal grill with an attached pedal-powered grinding wheel. His skill and artistic ability showed bright even on the small equipment. He was patient, caring, and precise as he showed us how to shape and bond metal. It seemed he was sharing the knowledge with us that he was deprived of sharing with his son. Some days Grandpa's pace was such, it seemed he was running out of time to share all he could possibly pass to Jack and me. Grandpa did say on occasion he thought we learned farm life and metal working much faster than Grandma's brothers. Oh, how I wished I could have been there on Lookout Mountain with him during his prime.

Much later in life, I realized my mom's older sister Vernon had never been a big part of our visits to the mountain. She had passed away before I had thought to ask why she chose not to visit. Was it only a coincidence, or did she have the same feelings as Uncle Carl? They had both spent most all their childhood there on Lookout Mountain.

One summer day, Grandpa said, "Now, you boys stay off of Shoemaker Hill!"

I asked, "What's happening up there, Grandpa?"

"They're cutting pulp wood, and it would be too dangerous for you two boys to be up there. A lot of equipment and men. Trees will be cut and falling in every direction. They will be burning the brush piles, and you might get hurt or burned." Later Jack and I discovered the real reason was that they were cooking moonshine up on Shoemaker Hill. I am sure Grandpa didn't want us there if the 'shiners were caught by the revenuers. Mostly he didn't want us to recognize any of the men involved. Somehow it seemed he was always thinking of our safety.

Grandpa probably got a few jars from the ol' still. He liked a good drink occasionally; Grandma called it his hooch. It, like a lot of things, was kept in the corn crib. I guess Grandpa liked his hooch guarded by the ol' bull snake.

Most of the area people were somehow involved in moonshine, whether it was selling supplies, making it, hauling it, or simply drinking it.

One summer I helped my dad in his auto repair and body shop. He would work over the engines, adding extra horsepower. When asked, he said the owner was a salesman and needed the extra power because of the load he carried. When I questioned the need for extra gas tanks, he replied the gas stations were hard for the salesman to locate on his travels.

Some of the cars were repainted quite frequently and usually a different color. At the time he was using lacquer paint, which only required a light sanding before painting. Two or three light coats of a new color and a light rubbing was all the work needed. Within half a day, the car was another color.

It was several years later when I finally realized my dad was rebuilding cars for the hauling of moonshine. Dad never drove himself, but some of the drivers later became quite famous on the NASCAR circuit.

I asked Grandpa one day if he could remember living with his dad in the mountains. He said he didn't remember much except things his dad had shown or told him. I asked when I would know about the Indian in me and when I would have the security of knowing I was Cherokee.

He replied with his smile, "You'll know when you can see yourself while looking up at the sky." It took me a long time to figure out the high cheekbones of the Cherokee was the clue. Now every time I look up, I see my cheekbones, and I am reminded of my heritage. Most of all I am reminded of Grandpa and his inspiration.

Toys and Games

Later that first summer, Grandpa showed us how to play roly-poly. He said it was also called Indian marbles. It was played by digging several holes six inches deep and about six feet apart. Clay or glass marbles were used as shooters. The object was to reach all the holes with your shooter. When you managed to get your shooter in a hole, you could shoot at your opponent in turn, knocking his marble out of the field of play. Grandpa said in the original game, his people used rock balls about three inches in diameter and played on a field about the size of a football field.

Roly-poly kept Jack and me occupied the whole summer. For several summers afterward, it was a hit with us. We even taught the game to other boys at school. It became a favorite marble game played at recess.

We could easily find old clay marbles along the creeks

or in the woods. Grandpa said they were sometimes used in the slingshots of his people.

He also said some people had called them mini balls, supposedly made by the Confederate solders for use when their lead ran out, but he knew this wasn't true. He said the clay would have broken, either inside the barrels or when it hit something in the woods.

He showed us how to make match shooters out of old clothespins. It was a simple task of reversing the clothespin's wooden side and notching a holding slot for the spring. A kitchen match was placed with the match head pointing into the spring. When the trigger was pulled, it would ignite the match and shoot it outward about ten feet.

Grandpa told us to never shoot the matches into grass or buildings. We usually saved the shooters for nighttime. The match looked like a flaming arrow when shot, and we always shot into the dirt area of the yard.

There was a large amount of fireflies along the roadways and fields of Dallas Hollow. One day Grandpa said, "Go get a couple of the broken canning jars, along with two of the old lids." When I came back up to the bench area, Grandpa told us if we caught enough fireflies to fill the jars, they would become lanterns, to be used for walking at night.

When nightfall came, we tried it and found it didn't work. We spent several hours catching lightning bugs but didn't have enough to cover the bottom of the jar. Later we realized it might have worked, but a quart jar of fireflies would have taken all summer to catch.

Another pleasure we had in the late afternoons was watching several flying squirrels play. After they climbed close to the tops of the hickory trees by the front bench and then jumped outward, they would stretch their legs in all directions, forming a sail from the flaps on each side. They'd ride the cooling air about two hundred feet and then hit the side of the barn. Upon impact, they would climb down and run back to the hickory trees. It seemed they never tired of the thrill of gliding on the cool summer air, and we never tired of watching.

One morning after breakfast and my chores, I went to sit with Grandpa on the bench. I noticed he was whittling on a small forked tree branch.

"What's this?" I asked.

Grandpa replied, "Go down to the barn and bring me the four strips of red rubber hanging on the hay door, along with the pair of my brogan shoes on the floor next to the tack room."

It was a puzzling request, but on my return to the bench, it soon became clear why the shoes and rubber were needed.

Grandpa took the shoes and cut the leather tongues from them, stating, "I was hoping these worn-out shoes could be of use and now they will be." He cut notches in the tongues and placed two strips of the red rubber into the notches, then wrapped the ends with waxed string. He cut notches on the tops of the forked hickory sticks, placing the other ends of the red rubber over the tips and wrapped them with string.

He said some people called it a slingshot, but his

people's slingshot didn't have the forked stick and was swung overhead.

"Now, never shoot toward people or buildings with this slingshot. Tonight go up on the road and flip small rocks at the bats."

When dusk came, Jack and I hurried to the roadway. Ole Blue followed and stood on guard. He watched our every move as if he knew Grandpa had given him his orders. We tried our new slingshots. To our amazement, the bats chased the stones. I guess the bats thought the stones were bugs. This became another source of entertainment for Jack and me on summer evenings.

When Grandpa was done with his work, he could usually be found on the front yard bench. Sometimes he would be sharpening his pocketknife on a whetstone he carried in his overalls. He would spit on the stone and move the knife blade in a slow circular motion. I thought he was surely going to grind the ol' blade into a small stub.

One such day Jack and I found several large, shiny green bugs. We brought one to Grandpa and asked what they were. With one of his smiles he said, "It's a June bug; go tell Grandma I said to give you some thread."

Upon my return to the bench he proceeded to tie the thread to one June bug leg and then threw the bug into the air. It circled his head for several minutes. Jack and I played with June bugs each time we located one. It was like having a small airplane on a string. Jack and I tried several types of bugs on a string, but none was ever as good as the green June bug.

During our first hog slaughtering, Grandpa came over to where Jack and I were standing, holding what looked like a wet balloon. He explained, "It's an Indian kick ball. It'll dry when you kick it in the dirt," and to our surprise, it did dry very rapidly, causing the outside to become leatherlike. Later Grandpa told us it was the hog's bladder blown up with air and tied with a knot. He said this was what he'd played with when he was little. Jack and I played with the Indian kick ball until it wore out.

Grandpa made us a couple of race spools. These were made using empty thread spools. A rubber band was placed through the hole and attached to a small stick on either side. Turning the spool would wind up the rubber band. Placing it on the floor and releasing the spool would cause the rubber band to unwind, propelling it across the floor. Jack and I received much pleasure playing with these during rainy or cold days and sometimes at night.

Grandpa let Jack and I go up on Shoemaker Hill one winter for snow sledding. We tried wooden sleds, and they were okay, but the fastest and most deadly of all was an old Ford hood from the 1940s. It was black and shiny; a small piece of chrome ran from the front all the way to the back.

We turned the hood upside down, and Jack and me plus a couple of neighbor boys loaded onto it. Someone gave a push and off we went, gaining speed at an incredible rate. We tried to slow down but to no avail. We even tried to steer sideways, but no-go. To our dismay, a large oak appeared straight ahead of us. We crashed into the tree. We managed to hit the tree with the side of the hood, causing the hood to spin, tumbling all of us out onto the snow. We were all okay but quite shaken. We never used a hood for a sled again.

We did find a couple of round saucer-shaped washing machine lids from wringer washers. They were fun because they allowed us to spin in circles while going downhill. One of the neighbor boys used his mother's washer top, and when he returned it she noticed it was scratched all over. Needless to say, he was grounded for quite some time.

Grandpa showed Jack and me how to make spin buttons. He took a large button and strung heavy thread through two opposing buttonholes. He made a loop about two feet in length and tied a knot in the thread. We held each end of the thread so the button sat in the middle, then spun the loop several times. When we pulled the ends of the loop outward, the button would spin with each pull of the thread.

One summer Grandpa built a small cart, which looked similar to his wagon, complete with a harness that fit the old male goat he called Billie. We were allowed to hook up Billie and ride around the property, in full control of the reins. Grandpa said, "Now, you can go anywhere around here, but keep the goat out of the garden. He'll eat the vegetables and tear up the garden." We managed to keep Ole Billie out of the garden, but he sure wanted to go in that direction sometimes.

One Sunday, my dad and one of my uncles were

visiting. After Sunday dinner they enjoyed a few twists of the bottle. They decided to see who was the strongest, and they went down to Ole Billie's pen and competed to see who could hold the goat's nose to the ground.

Jack and I didn't know what they had been doing and decided to harness Ole Billie up for a ride. When I grabbed him by the horns, he threw his head back swiftly, and one horn caught me just under my left eye. I bled quite heavily, and Jack ran up to the house, hollering that Ole Billie had hurt me bad. I was taken to the hospital, where several stitches were placed under my eye. Grandma said later the same night, "Now your grandpa was really upset to hear one of you boys got hurt. Why, he even told your dad and uncle there couldn't be any more drinking here."

Fall and Harvest

Fall arrived and brought corn and pumpkin harvest time. Grandpa took the mules and wagon out into the corn field. Jack got to ride in the wagon, and I walked alongside Grandpa and Grandma. We all broke the corn, still in husks, off the stalks, and threw them into the wagon.

After we had removed all the ears of corn, Grandpa cut the stalks with a sickle-like knife. He stacked the cut stalks into a teepee stack and tied the tops with twine.

He had planted pumpkins in the corn field. As we cleared a section of corn stalks, the pumpkins were exposed. We picked the pumpkins, and Grandpa placed them under the stacked corn stalks.

"Why are we hiding the pumpkins, Grandpa?" I asked.

"This way the frost or freeze can't hurt them," he replied. Later, when the pumpkins were removed from under the stalk teepees, we brought the corn stalks up to the barn shed and stored them for hog feed.

Grandpa always said, "If it's plant matter and we're done with it, then feed it to the hogs." He often reminded us that when it came to hogs, they'd eat anything. "So stay out of the pens, boys." I guess this was his way of keeping us safe around the hogs.

The picked corn was husked and fed through the manual corn kernel remover. Grandpa would pull the husk off the ears of corn, and Jack would feed the ears into the top of the kernel remover as I turned the handle. The corn kernels would drop into a feed sack below. It took a lot of ears of corn to fill a sack. The cobs fell onto the floor and were later stored under the shed with the husks. What corn didn't get shelled at this time was stored in the corn crib for chicken and livestock feed.

A few days after we shelled the corn, Grandma started a fire under the large kettle filled with water. When the water boiled, she added dry shelled corn and a small amount of lye.

I asked Grandpa what she was making.

"It's called hominy. Your grandma will can it when she's done cooking it," Grandpa said with his usual smile. Watching us learn about farm life appeared to please him.

We were allowed to stir the corn using Grandma's large wooden paddle. It was a slow cooking process. When the corn was ready, the outer skin of the kernels came lose. We helped carry water, which was used for rinsing the hominy. Later the same day Grandma canned the hominy and told us that the hominy would still require cooking when the cans were opened again.

When the fall gardens had all been picked and canned, usually green tomatoes, onions, and bell peppers remained on the plants. True to the country way, nothing went to waste. Grandma took all the remaining edible vegetables and prepared what she called chowchow. She diced the tomatoes, onions, and bell peppers, seasoned them, and placed the mixture into canning jars. It was a good condiment for winter foods. What was left before the frost came was fed to the hogs.

One clear, cool fall day Grandpa pulled his wagon out of the barn into the corn patch. He left it parked in between the corn stalk teepees about one-forth the way out in the field. I asked why the wagon was not in the barn as usual.

Smiling a larger than normal smile, he chuckled. "After supper tonight I'm going to show you boys some incredible sights."

After supper and chores, Grandpa Will gathered a couple of older quilts and took us down to the parked wagon. He spread the quilts out on the wagon then motioned to us to climb up. Ole Blue and Maggie, along with the rest of Grandpa's hunting dogs, all curled up under the wagon.

"Are we going to sleep out here?" I asked.

"No. Soon you'll see why we're here."

When dusk was complete, a glow started behind the

trees. As the glow got brighter and brighter, Grandpa exclaimed, "Here she comes, boys!"

A moon larger than we had ever seen poked out above the trees and ridge. It began bright orange, then faded to yellow as it rose into the clear, crisp night sky. Soon stars began to pop into sight as the night creatures began their nightly serenade. First were the whip-poor-wills, then the owls, and off in the distance we heard the fox and dogs, occasionally bringing a grunt from the pack below us.

Grandpa pointed out the constellation called the Big Dipper. He explained that this time of the year the Dipper was starting to turn so as to catch the water during the winter season. He told us early next spring the Dipper would turn again, releasing its catch, helping to water the earth during its growing season. We stayed for several hours, watching the sky and counting shooting stars.

I don't know who was most disappointed when we had to leave the field. Grandpa Will would probably have stayed there all night with us if it wouldn't have caused trouble with Grandma. He seemed to never get enough time to share his knowledge with us. Of course, Jack and I hung on his every word, waiting with great expectation to learn from Grandpa Will. We did manage to get in several more nights of sky watching before winter began. I believe if he had not met Grandma Ida, he would have preferred sleeping outdoors. We never felt unsafe or out of place when we were outdoors with Grandpa at night.

In the fall, Grandpa switched the four hogs he'd

picked out to be slaughtered over to the short pens. The short pens were smaller than the normal ones and had raised floors made of slab wood. Grandpa said keeping them there made them put on fat quicker and kept them from getting worms from the ground. All the rest of the years' hogs were sold, with the exception of his boar and next year's sow. Hog sales were how Grandpa earned some of his spare money.

A few weeks after the corn had been harvested, Grandpa loaded the wagon with all the shelled corn the wagon would hold. He had placed the shelled corn in sacks and staked them in rows. Once the chores had been completed after breakfast, he motioned for Jack and me to come get in the wagon.

"Where we going, Grandpa?" we both asked.

"We're going up to the gristmill at Greenpond. Your grandma has packed dinner for us. We'll be back this afternoon." Greenpond was about five miles away. It was the longest trip we had ever taken in the wagon. Grandpa told of wagon trips he had taken in the past. He said when he was a small boy he could remember the old growth forest, before most of it had been harvested. Grandpa told us with old growth trees, underlying brush didn't exist, allowing a wagon to travel without much of a roadway. He laughed and said, "The stories of white men blazing a trail were way overstated, since at the time much of the country was old growth forest or grasslands." He said some grasslands had been created by his people to make better hunting areas.

When we got there, the mill workers unloaded the wagon and weighed the corn. Grandpa and the mill manager worked the figures, and Grandpa was given several sacks of ground corn meal, flour, red sorghum seed, and a sack of lime. I asked why we left with what seemed less than we came with, and Grandpa explained they kept some for doing the milling.

Grandpa Will drove the wagon over to a stand of trees on the edge of the pond that powered the mill. The team seemed to enjoy the rest from the noonday sun under the shady trees. We sat by the pond and ate dinner. It was fascinating watching the water wheel turn, filling and emptying. This was our first visit, and after that, Grandpa arranged a walk-through tour of the mill. Grandpa beamed as he showed us all the workings of the grinding operations.

On the trip back, Jack climbed back on the meal sacks and soon was fast asleep. Grandpa began to smile as we made our way back home.

Watching Grandpa drive the team was a pleasure. He worked the reins with a relaxed effort. The team seemed to anticipate his every move or verbal command. I asked what the secret was to working a team.

Grandpa grinned and said, "It's the same for work stock, cattle, or dogs. You need their respect. You gain this from the tone of your voice, never hurting them, and only giving commands as needed. Once you do so, they will be waiting for your next command. It's like being the lead dog. If you pay attention, you'll see Ole Blue has the respect of all my other dogs. When he's around, all the others give him space and even let him eat first.

"Here, take the reins. Hold them relaxed and don't pull or move to one side. I'll give all the voice commands."

I did as Grandpa said and was in total amazement. The team seemed not to recognize who was holding the reins. "Why didn't they change when I started holding their reins?"

Grandpa chuckled and replied, "Remember we really didn't move the reins on them and they still heard my voice, so they didn't dare act up."

Grandpa and I talked the rest of the trip home. Jack and I both couldn't wait to get down off the wagon to tell Grandma of our day's adventure. Later I overheard Grandma say to Grandpa we were wound up like two magpies.

The apples were ready. We picked each tree clean. We placed the badly blemished apples in a container for hog feeding. Some of the apples were wrapped and placed in the corn crib to be eaten raw. What we didn't eat readily, Grandma peeled, cored, and cut into small pieces, placing them on linen sheets to dry in the sun. She turned the apple pieces daily.

After several days of drying, she wrapped the apple pieces in sacks and hung the sacks in the corn crib. I asked her why she didn't use the smokehouse instead, and she replied, "Everyone would think I'd burnt my pies because of the smoky flavor." She used the dried apples during the winter for pies and apple turnovers, which were our favorite winter snacks.

Fall also brought hog slaughter time, this fall being no different. One cool morning Jack and I watched as Grandpa and several neighbors took to the task. Each hog needed to be dipped into a barrel of hot water. This helped in removing the hair, which was scraped with knives. Ropes with pulleys and hooks were used for this task. Four good-sized hogs were split up this day. Grandpa kept two and each neighbor got one apiece. The hams, shoulders, and hocks were wrapped and placed in the smokehouse. Bellies and backs were cut into pieces for salt pork. The rest of the meat was ground up and made into sausage.

I was given the job of turning the hand-operated meat grinder. Grandma had cut up the pork into small pieces. She kept the grinder fed, while Grandpa positioned the sausage casings. After each casing was filled, he twisted each, tying small knots to make a long string of links. After all the sausage was prepared, the links were taken to the smokehouse and hung from the rafters, along with the hams and shoulders.

Inside the corn crib was a large box near one wall, raised up off the floor by a heavy post on each corner. It had deep sides with a cloth rolled down over it. The pork bellies and back pieces were placed inside the box between layers of coarse ground salt and left to cure.

Above the saltbox hung sacks filled with dried apples, along with bundles of sage and dill, while below the box peanuts were stacked for drying.

The fat from the pork was put into the large cast-iron kettle and cooked outside. Grandpa kept the fire going. He showed us how to keep the heat strong using a small flame. Flame, it seemed, could be very dangerous, as rendered fat was flammable. Grandma stirred and strained the small pieces of pork and skin out of the kettle. She called these pieces cracklings. Later that day, she mixed the cracklings into corn bread and called it crackling bread. It was quite the hit at supper.

When the fat had cooked into a clear liquid, Grandma said it was ready. The liquid was dipped and poured through linen into five-gallon buckets with lids. Grandma told us it was called lard as soon as it turned an angel-white color.

The next day Grandpa fired up the smokehouse. What a sight for small eyes to behold! I was sure Grandpa had made a mistake and set the building on fire. Soon there was smoke coming out of every crack.

After several minutes, Grandpa smiled and quietly said, "Now don't you worry. It takes a lot of smoke to cure the hams."

Grandpa used an old iron stove to make the smoke. The stovepipe went into the smokehouse and turned down toward the floor. A bucket with water was placed under the bottom pipe opening. The water bucket was there in case any sparks came through the pipe. He said he didn't want to catch the smokehouse on fire.

Grandpa selected the wood. He used only hickory and then only certain pieces. He liked the greener pieces for stoking the fire, because they produced more smoke.

At night he would fill the stove and turn the damper down. He said this way he didn't have to come out too many times at night to stoke it.

The smokehouse fired for several days. When Grandpa shut down the smoker, Jack and I would go check out the bounty of the season. Ham and shoulders, along with endless strings of sausage, hung from the rafters. The aroma was unforgettable. Many seasons of use had saturated the interior boards of the smokehouse with the aroma of smoked hickory and meats. Each year, it seemed Grandpa had made way more than we could possibly eat. By springtime, most had been consumed.

If Grandpa could find a good supply of pecans, he would lay the shelled pecans on a flat pan inside the smokehouse. He salted the nuts and turned them frequently during smoking time. Afterward the nuts were placed in canning jars and sealed. They were in great demand during holidays.

I had thought Grandpa had made more sorghum than usual for us earlier one fall but would understand more when we made our fall trip to the mill with the corn. Grandpa loaded the usual corn sacks onto the wagon but also brought several buckets of sorghum with us. When we loaded for the return trip I noticed two large sacks, which were not corn meal, flour, or feed.

As we pulled the team out onto the road, I asked Grandpa what was in the sacks. He said, "Why, it's moonshine sugar!"

"We going to start moonshining, Grandpa?" I asked.

This brought quite a laugh. "No, moonshine sugar

is cheaper than regular sugar because it's coarser. Your grandma doesn't care because as she uses it, most of it's boiled, like in jam, preserves, pies, cobblers, and even sweet tea. She has a small grinder she uses to make it finer if needed."

When we arrived home Jack asked what we got, and Grandpa smiled and said, "Oh, the usual—corn meal and sugar." He seemed to know I was busting at the seams to tell Jack what we really got and explain the difference.

Soon school started. I had to catch a school bus, and the bus stop was about half mile away. The first week or so Grandpa walked most of the way with me. He said it was for my safety, but I think he enjoyed the time with me. I caught the bus in front of Grandpa's daughter Vernon's house. It gave me time to visit my cousins. Sometimes Grandpa and Jack would be at Vernon's when the bus returned. He timed his visit there so as to catch all his grandkids coming home from school. I was able to see Grandpa's tender side as he visited with the girls.

When he was finished visiting with Vernon's kids, Grandpa, Jack, and I would walk home. Not attending school did give Jack more quality time at home with Grandpa while I was gone. But I also knew Grandpa was eager to have us both back under his wing for the night. Grandma did not lack concern and admiration for Jack and me. She was anxious to greet me on my return from school, usually with a big hug and a smile. And of course, she made sure I was clean, well fed, and dressed properly when I left in the mornings. It was most often Grandma who checked to see if I had my school supplies and homework for the day.

Within a couple of years, Jack was attending school too. Grandpa tried to not show he missed us during the day, but I knew better. When we walked down the drive to the house, he would always be in the front yard on his bench. With a big smile, he would ask how school was. Then after we had changed clothes and finished our homework, he would accompany us while we did our chores.

One year, about three weeks after school started, I walked out to do morning chores and noticed my new bicycle was missing. I asked if Grandpa or Jack had moved it. They both came out and looked but to no avail.

Grandpa walked over, placed an arm around my shoulders, and said, "It was probably too nice a bike for Dallas Hollow. Someone was too envious of what you had and took it. It must have been someone from around here, or else the dogs would have raised all kind of cane last night."

I never recovered the bike. It was difficult thinking someone I knew would do such a thing. If someone in Dallas Hollow took it, they either buried it or moved it out of there.

I soon started enjoying my old bicycle again, the one I had learned to ride on. The driveway at Grandpa's place was dirt, covered with cinders. Grandpa Will still enjoyed the warmth of coal burned in the pot-bellied stove. The ashes were emptied on the drive and raked smooth.

While I was learning to ride, I must have crashed at least a hundred times. Not many body parts were immune to scrapes or bruises.

The fall was filled with the normal harvesting tasks. Hominy making and canning and drying of fruit were ongoing. Sorghum making meant the gathering of neighbors and a chance to listen to the men tell stories around the vat. Sometimes they told of hunting adventures or news of their family members. Either way it was fascinating to Jack and me. We were aware of Grandma and the neighbor women quilting, but as Grandpa said, "They don't bother us when we're visiting, and we give them their space."

The black-eyed peas had been picked weeks before and placed in large sacks. For several nights we sat around the pea sacks and shelled peas in the kitchen. The pea hulls were placed under the shed for later use as hog food. We had picked the peas in ol' man Shoemate's field. He was getting pretty old by now—still able to plow and plant but unable to do much of the picking.

Grandpa had agreed we would pick and shell the peas and split the harvest. I had learned Grandpa and the neighbors shared a lot of crops. The Shoemates still had milk cows and churned butter. Grandpa grew extra crops and traded for their milk and butter. He always liked fresh milk and butter better than the store-bought milk. He would eat oleo but preferred real butter.

Winter and Holidays

As the winter season came, it brought a complete change to our routines and daily life. After I got home from school, it was chore time, then homework, before supper. This reversal was due to shorter daylight, because it was better to do chores in the daylight. During the winter season, the house was filled with the rewards of the harvest. Blackberry cobbler and apple turnovers were my favorite desserts. Grandma always had a stack of apple turnovers close to the stove. She would give us one apiece as soon as we came home. Grandma would say, "You boys need plenty of energy to do your chores."

Holidays meant the smoked hams and sweet potatoes would be served, and lots of family would visit. The kitchen table usually had eight to ten people around it, mostly relatives, but sometimes neighbors came. Winter was one of the times during the year we ate with so many at the table. Since the table was full of adults, the small children sat at a smaller table or were allowed to eat in the living room. Other cooks brought dishes, and we had every food one could imagine at those meals. Grandpa would say, "My hunting dogs are going to eat well tonight." He knew there would always be an abundance of table scraps after meals such as these.

There was an art to cooking on a wood cookstove. Grandma had mastered the stove during her sixty-plus years of continual use of wood. The aroma was different; the wood smoke mixed with the smells given off by the foods. I still think foods taste better when prepared this way. Maybe the fact that these were fresh foods, grown with organic fertilizers, without preservatives, made a difference too. Of course, the gentle warmth given off by the stove was also to be cherished, especially during the winter months.

Winter meals were different in many ways. During the summer, when sweet corn was in season, Grandma would have us pick the corn only minutes before she cooked it. I remember asking why I couldn't pick it Sunday before church. She said it lost its sugar and started to mold if picked too early. Grandma would give me the choice to pick corn or pluck chicken feathers. I'd take corn picking over chicken plucking anytime.

During the winter season, meals were prepared with canned, salted, dried, or smoked foods. There wasn't much fresh chicken beside an occasional stewing hen, which needed feathers removed. This was a chore Jack and I were usually given. Dipping chickens into boiling water to release the feathers creates a very distinctive smell. I sure don't miss cleaning chickens in that manner today, but the smell would trigger fond memories of the years with Grandpa Will.

The first year with Grandpa, Christmas season was special. A few days before Christmas Grandpa said, "Get your coats and follow me." We stopped and retrieved a small saw and hatchet and then proceeded up into the woods.

"Where we going, Grandpa?" asked Jack, but I knew it was Christmas tree time, and I tried not to show my excitement. Grandpa smiled and said, "Oh, the house needs some greenery. Santa's coming soon, and we wouldn't want him to catch us with our pants down, would we?"

Jack and I both were both surprised when Grandpa pointed at a cedar tree, which looked like it came out of a wish book. Grandpa said, "Why don't you two look up in the trees and find some mistletoe, and I'll cut the tree."

We spotted some on a lower limb. After he was finished cutting the tree, Grandpa cut down a small pole with the hatchet. With little effort he retrieved the mistletoe from the tree. We were certainly all grins when we got our haul back to show Grandma.

Grandpa made a stand for our tree by nailing two boards about two feet long to the bottom of the tree, placed in a cross arrangement for stability. He trimmed any limbs that were not needed and placed the tree on its stand in the living room.

Grandma had popped popcorn while we were gone.

She took out a needle and thread and helped us string popcorn and decorate the tree. Grandpa had a pot-bellied stove in the living room. We did not have a mantel to hang our stockings, so Grandma put them on the wall behind the stove.

The mistletoe was hung over the door. Grandma made hot chocolate from canned cocoa for us as we sat around the radio listening to Christmas music. Grandpa had placed a metal pot on the pot-bellied stove and filled it with peanuts. He shook the pot every few minutes to keep the peanuts from burning. Nothing's better than roasted peanuts and hot chocolate on a cold winter's night.

The next week Grandma kept busy making different kinds of cookies and holiday sweets. Every day, Jack and I were treated to several new types of cookies. It seemed we were the designated tasters. Grandma wore a large smile during all of our first Christmas season. For Jack and me, she took on the image of Mrs. Santa Claus. Her cheeks somehow seemed to have more color. There was always a plate of hot apple turnovers, along with tins of cookies and fudge and most every kind of nut, along with fresh citrus Mom and Dad brought over.

The first year, and for several more, Jack and I were part of the Christmas pageant at the local church. Most often we were two of the wise men or shepherds. The costumes were usually simple but effective. Most of the community would attend the pageant. Small paper bags with fruits and small toys were passed out to all the kids after the event.

Christmas arrived with toys and clothes for Jack and myself. I received from Mom and Dad a fishing rod and reel, along with a fish gig. Grandpa promised we would try out both the next summer.

A few weeks after that first Christmas, it started to snow one morning. Grandpa seemed to acquire a perk in his step, and he wore a slight grin most of the day. He told us it looked like we were in for a good snowfall.

We accomplished our chores during the day, but more slowly because of the snow. At supper Grandpa said, "Well, you boys are in for a treat soon as we finish here."

After supper Grandpa took two dish pans and said, "Come on down to the shed area with me." Jack and I were really puzzled by then.

We asked, "What're we going to get out here?" Grandpa scraped the top layer off the snow and filled both pans to heaping with the fresh snow.

"Here, you two—take these pans back in to Grandma. She'll show you what to do with it." Grandpa grinned from ear to ear as we walked back to the house.

Grandma took the pans. Into the smaller one she poured vanilla, sugar, eggs, and cream. She gave each of us one of her large wooden spoons and told us to stir. Soon the snow mixture turned to a familiar consistency. "Now it's ready. It's called snow cream," Grandma said as she readied the bowls.

Grandpa continued to grin from ear to ear as we all enjoyed the snow cream around the pot-bellied stove. Although this was our first snow cream, it was not our last. Jack and I were usually quite ready when the first snowfall of the season came. I don't know who was the most excited at snow cream season, Grandpa or us.

One Christmas after the power had been installed, Grandpa got a special gift from Dad. It was a small Emerson TV, with a small black and white viewing screen in a Bakelite case. Dad helped put up an antenna, and soon we were watching TV for the first time.

It was as fascinating for Grandpa as it was for Jack and me. Maybe it was his Indian heritage, because Grandpa's favorite programs on TV were wrestling and baseball. Slowly TV overtook radio as the evening entertainment, adding another flickering light to the nights in Dallas Hollow.

There weren't many programs, and our antenna pulled in only one station. Before the programs were due to be broadcast, the TV would be turned on. We would watch what was called a test pattern. Sometimes Grandpa would adjust knobs for better picture clarity. After the TV was turned off, we would watch the picture become a small bright dot before disappearing.

One particular winter season started out like all the others, with cold nights. Grandma's good home cooking, followed by the usual desserts, topped the supper menu. The evenings were always filled with baths, homework, and listening to the radio.

One night, screams interrupted the normal sounds, accompanied by an orange light shining on the widows. Grandpa jumped up and said, "Something's burning."

And we all went outside to see. The neighbor's house was completely engulfed by flames. The family was visible against the fire's bright glow. I saw some folks throwing buckets of water toward the house. Soon flames were shooting skyward, and everyone settled back, away from the flames and heat.

"Stay here! I'll go over and make sure everyone's okay." We watched patiently waiting for Grandpa's return and the news. When he got back, Grandma asked, "Did everyone make it out before it burned?"

Grandpa replied, "Yes, all are okay. The old man was still pretty drunk when I got there. He probably put too much wood in the stove and left the damper wide open. Anyway, it'll be a while before he sits around the stove drunk again. The house is a total burn. Ida, you might want to go over tomorrow and see if we can help with blankets or food." He said Jack and I could probably be of help with the cleanup.

Winter seasons came and went, with the usual good food and hunting trips. We did see our first bobcat one season. Grandpa always told tales of panthers and their screams, but we never saw one while we were living in Dallas Hollow.

Grandpa also talked of ring-tailed cats. We never saw any of those around our part of country. Later, I checked resources and found out they indeed existed but usually in the mountains of the West. I still have no idea how he knew about them except through his people.

He told us about how Grandma's younger brother

had received his head injury. He said, "It wasn't long after the flu had taken your grandma's dad. Her brother decided to prove his manhood. He was about your age and kind of cocky.

"Well, one night he went hunting with the dogs. A panther started screaming, and he began running for the house. He struck a low limb in his blind run. Most of us didn't think he would pull through. It left the big scar on his forehead.

"Let this tale be a lesson for you two boys. If you hear an ol' panther start to scream, don't panic and run. You might run straight into a limb or, worse, the ol' panther's mate. Remember, it's not the one you hear but the one you don't hear that can be the most dangerous."

He tried to instill this idea in us, especially regarding snakes. The one you see usually was no threat because you could avoid getting bitten, but the one that is well-hidden bites.

Those lessons must have worked well for Jack and me. We were all over the woods and creeks while living with Grandpa, and we managed to avoid getting bitten.

Spring and Planting

Spring came, and it was planting time again. One morning as Grandpa was preparing the team for plowing, he said, "Today I'm getting the hill ready for sorghum and popcorn. I hope the weather doesn't get too hot and make the popcorn pop before we get to it." I noticed he wore a smile, but Jack said, "How'll we get to it before the birds eat it all?" I smiled, and Grandpa knew he'd only fooled one of us.

Often Jack and I would go to a high point on the hillside. Blue and Maggie and sometimes Maggie's new pups would tag along. We would watch Grandpa Will get the fields ready to plant. On occasion Grandma brought us snacks there on the hillside. I thought it was a chance to watch Grandpa work the earth. He used the mules around the edges of the fields. Mules, we were told, did not spook when they disturbed a yellow jacket nest. Grandpa told us that yellow jackets often built their nests in holes left by decaying tree roots. Once the field edges had been properly prepared, the mules were taken back to the barn.

Next came the large work team. Discs, plows, and harrows were employed. As we watched from afar, it seemed as if Grandpa was combing the earth. Dark strings of earth looked like hair, especially when he started on the hillsides, making soft curves around the slopes. Then I would remember Grandpa referring to the earth as Mother Earth. It made sense he would have taken great pride in combing Mother Earth's hair. This was one of many ways Grandpa showed his deep Indian roots.

All kinds of birds would follow Grandpa as he turned the fields. They seemed to enjoy the fruits of plowing. Grandpa would smile and say, "The birds eat all the grubs and bad worms. If it wasn't for their appetite we would lose a lot of our crops." Grandpa never minded the birds in his fields. He said the birds ate more insects than fruits and vegetables. Once he stated, "Now, when you see a bird on an ear of corn, the bird's not eating corn—he's eating the silkworm."

We were all employed when crop planting came about. Thinning the corn, planting squash, potatoes, onions, and green beans, along with settings, all had to be done by hand. Several weeks were required for these tasks. Grandma had started some plants early, such as the tomato plants. Grandpa had made her a heat box, he called it, from a couple of windows hinged together over a wooden box. The windows allowed sun to heat the soil, enabling an early start for the tender plants.

The first spring Grandpa introduced us to poke salad. We walked along the fence lines, and Grandpa pointed to the plants with red stems. He said, "Now, the young leaves are okay to eat after your grandma cooks them. Don't ever eat them raw, especially the berries. You can play with the berries. My people used them for color dying. They're a pretty color blue. In most cases, the prettier the color, the more dangerous it is."

We asked what he meant when he compared color to danger.

Grandpa replied, "Take coral snakes, butterflies, beetles, Gila monsters, and caterpillars; they all look pretty, but none are any good to eat, so don't try. Most are poisonous and can kill you with their bite. Nature will give you plenty of notice; you need to heed her warnings."

At supper Grandma cooked the poke salad we had picked. She boiled it with salted pork strips and served it with sliced hard-boiled eggs on top. It tasted a little like spinach or collard greens.

Grandma planted bib lettuce, green onions, and radishes in the early garden beds. These beds were on the south side of the barn next to Grandma's starter boxes. Grandpa told us he had put them there to gain warmth from the sun shining on the barn in early spring. The beds quickly produced edible crops. Grandma would make a salad called wilt salad: lettuce, onions, and radishes with hot bacon grease poured over them before serving. We ate a lot of wilt salad every spring before the other crops started coming in.

Springtime also brought crops like new potatoes and carrots, always a favorite in stews. The spinach and chard were cool season risers, and so were the snap sweet peas. As soon as the tomato plants put on green tomatoes, it meant one of Grandpa's favorites—fried green tomatoes. It seemed at times Grandma had prepared way more fried green tomatoes than we could eat. The huge platters were usually eaten at one setting, however, leaving few scraps.

The setting hens had all hatched their first rounds of chicks, and soon the young fryers meant fresh fried chicken again, which also meant we would have chicken gravy instead of sausage gravy. Somehow, chicken gravy tasted better with fresh spring vegetables.

One of our first encounters with chicken snakes happened one spring. Grandma Ida mentioned at supper that some of the new chicks in the brood pen had been disappearing, so we should watch for anything crawling around the pen the next day. She said Blue and Maggie were raising cane around the chicken pen in the mornings.

"What did Grandma mean by something crawling around the pen?" I asked Grandpa the next morning.

"Well, she suspects a chicken snake," Grandpa replied.

"How will we know if it's a chicken snake?"

"I'll set out by the hen house with you today. If it's a chicken snake it won't take long to show up. They can't resist the taste of chicken."

Grandpa took a hoe and a chair down to the chicken

pen, and we settled down next to the hen house. We were there about an hour when Grandpa said, "Look over there on the back side of the brood pen." The brood pen was full of newly hatched chicks. At first I didn't see anything but chicks. Then what looked like a small limb about three inches in diameter and four to five feet long began to move. It had two enlarged humps along its side, which I learned later were recently consumed chicks.

"It's a snake, Grandpa!" I shouted as Grandpa walked toward the pen with his hoe. I stood as if in a trance. I could not believe a snake could reach such a size. After Grandpa dispatched the snake, I asked why we had not noticed it around the yard. He told us this kind of snake had special scales and spent most of the time in trees searching for birds. Grandpa told us not to worry about being bitten by this type, as they were nonpoisonous and only visited when new chicks were present. We spent a lot of time for many summers looking upward when we were under the trees.

Grandpa told us that chicken snakes and raccoons were both mostly night hunters. He said, "Both take advantage of sleeping prey. The coon will go to a squirrel's nest at night and raid the small squirrels. The snake raids the roosting areas and nests for sleeping birds."

In a few days, Grandpa took us down to the shed area of the barn. Maggie was on a straw bed Grandpa had prepared for her. She had given birth to a litter of pups. This was the first time Jack and I were around newborn pups. Maggie was gentle and allowed us to be quite close. When I noticed how small the pups were, it became clear why Maggie had been so concerned about the chicken snake. She must have understood her pups would have been only a snack to a snake of that size.

Grandpa had prepared a special food mix containing raw eggs. He said Maggie needed the mix to produce good milk for the pups. Jack and I learned soon that Grandpa also liked raw eggs. He would poke a small hole in the shell and suck out the egg. When we questioned this way of eating eggs, he said it was like enjoying the taste of raw eggs in eggnog or the snow cream we had enjoyed the winter before.

We learned Grandpa liked okra, but not fried—he preferred it stewed. Grandma always prepared a bowl of stewed okra for Grandpa when she made fried okra. Grandpa had another unusual quirk with his coffee. He liked using a regular coffee cup and saucer and would pour the coffee into the saucer, then sip from the saucer. He said drinking coffee this way brought out the flavor.

In the early spring when the new piglets were weaned and starting out on their own, Grandpa called us down to the hog pens. "Now, I've got the pigs separated from the sow. You boys climb in with the piglets. Catch one and hold it still." We held the pigs, and Grandpa proceeded to put rings into their noses with what looked like a pair of pliers.

I asked, "What are the rings for?"

Grandpa replied, "The rings keep the pigs from rooting with their noses. Why, if these weren't on their noses, they would dig up the dirt deep enough to crawl out under the pen. The rings hurt their noses when the pigs try rooting. They only try to dig a couple of times, and then they learn it's best to stay in the pen."

Spring was the time for Grandma's deep house cleaning. The temperature was warm enough to open the house. Floor scrubbing was a big item at this time of year. The rugs were hung outside and beaten. This released the deep dust from the winter wear. Jack and I helped beat the rugs. It was one of the only times we could hit household items and not get into trouble.

Grandma Ida used this time to wash all the winter wear and quilts. Clotheslines were heavily laden with winter wear. When they were dry, she packed them away until the next cold season.

Grandpa took this time of year to move the outhouse. He had planned the move very cleverly. Each year the outhouse was moved approximately eight feet forward or to the side. A new hole was dug. The dirt from the new hole was used to fill in the old hole. Some years this meant the outhouse was eight feet closer to the house. Being closer was not a bad thing when you had to go in a hurry, which usually meant you were feeling sick.

Fence rebuilding and relocation was a springtime chore. Post holes had to be dug. Grandpa said the ground was easier to work at this time of year. He told us how Ol' Man Winter had beaten the soil with his ice and freezing temperatures, making spring thaw the perfect time to dig. I asked why he didn't use the hard woods like oak or hickory instead of cedar for the fence post. He explained that even though the cedar was softer, it was not susceptible to insects or rot. He showed us how to place a rock at the bottom of the fence-post hole. He said this provided drainage and made the post more stable.

Grandpa said his teams seemed to have a perkier step in the spring. He reckoned it was because they'd had their winter rest, plus the cooperative condition of the soil. Of course the still-cool weather helped the teams. I had noticed after the teams came back to the barn they were not as lathered as summer. This was a good thing because it meant less time washing and brushing them down.

Cleaning out the chicken house was done this time of year. Let me tell you, that was one stinky job. Chicken houses are dark, with several rows of rousting rails, which resemble small bleachers in a stadium. There were always more rousting rails than the number of chickens. It's difficult removing the manure from under the rousting rails, as some are close to the ground. Grandpa would say, "The chicken house was for chickens only." Thank goodness a door gave us access.

The horse and goat pens were cleaned daily year around. The manure from these pens had been piled beside the barn. All the manure was managed and placed either on the garden or fields before planting. Grandpa usually mixed the manures before spreading. He said chicken manure used straight was too hot for most plants, meaning it burned the plants and caused them to wither.

Clotheslines were restrung or tightened. Grandpa

showed us how to adjust the tightening wire that held the cross arms. After the cross arms were secured, we would adjust the clotheslines themselves. We learned that wire clotheslines shrank in the winter and became looser in the summer. In the spring we tightened the wire, while fall meant loosening them.

A couple of years after Jack and I moved in with Grandpa, I was picking vegetables with Grandma. I noticed she seemed happier than normal.

"Grandma, you seem mighty happy," I piped.

"I was thinking about how full of joy the house has been since you and Jack moved in. It's nice having laughter back. Your grandpa even said it was like having his boys back. He can barely wait to share time with you two. I'm always happy if I see my Indian smiling. After the disappointments Will has been through, it's a pleasure seeing him happy again. Again, don't share this with anyone else, especially your grandpa," she said with a quick wink.

I knew she had shared something very special. It felt good knowing she trusted me in such a manner. I was puzzled by her comment about Grandpa's disappointments but knew better than to question Grandma. I knew when she felt it was time she might share more information with me.

Hunting

Not too long after our first Christmas with Grandpa, he took Jack and me down to the barn work area. "We're about out of the good cuts of pork, and I don't know about you boys, but I'm kind of tired of stewing hens. I've got a craving for rabbit."

"Does this mean we're going hunting?" I asked eagerly. I was hoping Grandpa would let me shoot one of his guns.

"Well, in a way, but not the way you're thinking. When you startle rabbits or any other type of game and they run before they're shot, it causes the meat to taste strong. I'm going to teach you both how to build a rabbit gum. Hold your arm out," Grandpa said, and he measured my arm from under my armpit to my wrist.

"Why are you measuring my arm?"

"I need to build the rabbit gum to fit your arm."

"You're not going to put me in the gum, are you?"

Grandpa laughed loudly. "No, I'm not putting you into the gum. I needed the correct length to ensure you could reach the rabbit. If I made the gum too long, you couldn't remove the caught rabbit."

Grandpa took some of the slab boards usually used on the hog pens and cut them to the measurements he had taken from my arms. He nailed them together, making a box with both ends open. He trimmed the raw edges with a draw knife.

On one end he nailed chicken wire, and on the other he fitted narrow strips for slides onto each side. He then made a board that fit the slide opening. A stick with a forked top was mounted on the top about two-thirds of the way back. He drilled a hole a small distance behind the stick. He fashioned a stick with a notch and placed it into the hole behind the forked stick. Another stick was cut, barely long enough to reach from the front slide door to the notched stick. Grandpa connected the slide door to the top stick and also to the notched stick with string.

"There now, this is a fine gum." He proceeded to rub horse manure all over the door and inside the gum.

We asked in unison, "What's the stink for?"

He explained it was to cover up our scents to avoid spooking the rabbits.

When he finished, we walked out to the woods on the side of the old corn field. Grandpa placed the gum into some small brush slightly off what he said was a rabbit trail. He placed some bits of carrots and cabbage inside, behind the trigger stick, and raised the trap door, locking the trigger stick with the notch he'd cut into the stick.

"Grandpa, why do you call it a gum?" I asked.

"Well, my people made them from blackgum trees. Blackgum trees have hollow limbs and trunks. They would only have to make a trap door for the opening to the hollow part. When they used this method to trap rabbits it was called a rabbit gum."

He built two more of the gums and placed them along different paths. He told us to check the gums every morning. Sure enough, about twice a week at least one of the gums would have a rabbit in it.

Until we got older, Grandpa always went down to the gums and took care of killing and preparing the rabbits. Later, Jack and I would take care of the rabbits ourselves. In the spring we ate quite a bit of fried rabbit, and I had to admit the rabbits we trapped tasted better than any we shot with guns.

I asked why he'd placed the chicken wire on the back end of the gum. He smiled and said there were two reasons, the first being not to scare the rabbit after the door came down. It allowed the rabbit to still see outside. The second was it enabled us to see what had been trapped.

"You know, ol' skunks like greens and carrots too!" he said with a larger than normal grin.

I slept with anticipation the first night. When breakfast was finished and our chores were done, we walked down to the rabbit gums. The first two were still armed; a quick look showed the bait had not been disturbed. As soon as I saw the last gum, I knew we had something inside. The trap door had been tripped. I ran to the back side and knelt, peering in through the chicken wire.

"It's a rabbit!" I shouted in excitement.

Grandpa laughed loudly and said, "I'm glad it was a rabbit. Remember what I said yesterday about skunks. If you had put your nose any closer looking into the gum and an ol' skunk was in there, you would have to sleep in the corn crib for several days. Grandma wouldn't let you in the house stinking like a skunk."

Grandpa said, "If we need the rabbits, it's okay to take them. When we have all the meat we need, then you need to release the rabbits from the gums. Trip the triggers and leave them alone until we need them again. This is the way with all things. Take whatever is needed, whether it be animal or crops, but nothing more. When you live this way, there'll always be something left for those in need."

He told Jack and me how his dad trapped turkeys. He said they dug a long trench about four feet deep, sloped at both ends, and covered the trench with small limbs. The trench opening was in the center, and one end of the trench was surrounded by briars on the top and sides. Then they baited the trench with corn. When the turkeys followed the corn trail, they would end up in the center of the briar cage. When the turkeys had eaten all the grain, it was natural for them to pace along the outside perimeters of the cage. They never seemed to go back to the center where the entrance was located; thus they remained trapped.

We laughed when he told us the time when he was about our age and he decided to crawl into the cage and retrieve a turkey that had been trapped. He said the turkey pecked and clawed him so bad it looked like he had run through the briars himself—there wasn't any place on his body that didn't have a scratch. It gave us a warm feeling to know our grandpa had been much like us when he was younger.

He shared the story of snipe hunting: the practice of enticing a gullible person to go out at night and hold a bag open while several others chased the "snipes" into the bag. Grandpa tried to ensure we would not be this gullible. He said this was where the expression "left holding the bag" came from.

That year I received a Daisy BB gun for my birthday. Grandpa looked it over and said, "Should be a good starter gun for you boys. Don't shoot at any chickens or livestock. Crows, hawks, and snakes are all okay to shoot, but leave the songbirds alone. Remember, the Creator placed them here for our enjoyment, not as food. If I catch you shooting at them, then it will be your supper you have killed."

Jack and I shot at a few crows and hawks, and also an occasional snake. Target practice was our main focus. We must have broken a hundred or more Watkins medicine bottles. I now wish I had those bottles, as they have become quite collectable.

I learned a lesson about not taking anything that

didn't belong to me. I was out of ammo for my BB gun and had spotted a half dollar on Grandma's dresser. I took the money and bought the ammo. I intended to repay the money, but Grandma noticed it was missing before I had the chance to replace it. When Grandpa heard about what had happened, he had quite a conversation with me. He said since the money didn't even belong to Grandma—it had been collected at church for a missionary cause—I needed to repay it tenfold.

That half dollar cost me five dollars. It took me quite some time working odd jobs to earn the money for repayment. Before I had earned enough to repay Grandma, I realized my grandpa's Indian method of punishment was sometimes harder than being spanked with a belt. Sure, the belt leaves welts, but the next day all was forgotten. But this approach made me think about my one wrongdoing for a lifetime. I still drop money into the offering plates of churches and remember this lesson. It's a dual-purpose memory, highlighting both a lesson from my childhood and the compassion of my grandpa.

One spring day I told Grandpa I sure would like a shotgun of my own. He said, "Why don't you go down to the cemetery office and ask about mowing the grass in the cemetery this summer?" So I worked most of the summer mowing grass in the mornings. I not only made enough money for a new 16-gauge shotgun but also enough for a shiny new Schwinn bicycle. The bike was nice, but every time I rode it all I could think of was going hunting with my own shotgun.

Hunting season came, and Grandpa said, "Why don't we go out and try out the new gun of yours?"

"Where we going?" I said with excitement.

"Up on Shoemaker Hill and out past the hay fields. I saw several coveys of quail there yesterday."

We walked along with two of Grandpa's blue tick hounds beside us. When we entered the field, Grandpa said, "Now, I'm going to give the dogs a whistle and they'll started working the field. Walk behind the dogs, and when they stop, get your gun ready. The quail will flush and probably turn to our left or right. If it's to the right, it's your shot, and if it's to the left it's mine. Any birds that fly straight ahead are fair game to both of us. This way we won't shoot each other."

Suddenly Maggie stopped. My heart pounded with anticipation as the quail took flight with thundering wings. As soon as they were about six feet above the ground, they turned to the left.

I saw Grandpa raise his gun and fire two rapid shots. He had fired both barrels of the 12-gauge, dropping about four birds. Once we had gathered the birds, Grandpa gave another whistle and the dogs started working the field again. It wasn't long before Blue and Maggie stopped again. This time the flush was mine. I fired and only managed one bird, but I didn't care because it was my first kill with the new gun. Grandpa and I managed several more hunts that fall. It was always a treat watching those two dogs work the fields as a team.

After I was fourteen years of age, my dad and I

hunted on Lookout Mountain at my Grandma Ida's parents' place. Her brother and mom still lived there. It was a setting out of the past. When Dad took us hunting there, Grandpa Will would never come with us. He always seemed to have something that needed to be done at his place. I never asked him why he didn't like going out on the mountain, as I remembered my conversations with Grandma Ida.

One year in the fall, Grandpa gathered his dogs and took Jack and me down to the creek.

Jack asked, "What are we going to do here, catch fish with the dogs?"

Grandpa grinned and said, "No, I'm going to give them some exposure to game. Why, I bet there's at least one ol' coon down here at the creek."

It wasn't long before we came upon a log that had fallen across the creek. Sure enough, about a third of the way out on the log stood a fat ol' coon. The coon just stood there as we approached. Grandpa turned to the dogs and let out a loud whistle. The dogs took up the scent and ran out onto the log where the coon was. There was quite a scuffle, which ended with another of Grandpa's whistles. The coon had been torn to shreds, with various parts in and out of the water.

I asked why the coon didn't run when the dogs approached. He told us the day before he had come down and drilled a hole in the log, then driven several horseshoe nails into the log surrounding the hole. The nails were angled toward the center of the hole, and Grandpa put a marble in the bottom of the hole.

He said, "Now, a coon's a curious critter. When he reaches into the hole to get the marble, his paw passes the nails. When he tries to remove it, the nails keep him there."

I said, "Wasn't that kind of cruel?"

Grandpa explained if the ol' coon on the log had managed to get his young dogs into the water today, only the coon would have come back to shore. He said in the water, a coon would climb up on a dog's head and drown the dog. "Maggie and Blue are smart enough not to chase the coon into the water, but the pups needed a head start. When it comes to a coon or my hunting dogs, I'm going to give an edge to my dogs if I can." He smiled and called the dogs for our return home.

Later the same day we walked past the cemetery and came upon a large white oak tree. Grandpa pointed up to a large hole between two limbs. "Now, climb up there to the hole and reach down into it. There'll probable be an ol' opossum in there. Grab him and throw him down. The dogs will have a lot of fun with him."

I climbed up, limb by limb, finally reaching the hole. When I reached down into the hole, I felt something, but it didn't feel like a possum. I pulled my hand out and suddenly a screech owl was buzzing around me. My whole world became louder and louder. The dogs were going crazy with excitement. I could barely hear Grandpa give the command whistle as he tried to calm them.

Grandpa said, "You better get down out of there— that ol' owl's plenty mad." It seemed like it took forever to descend, with the owl close behind. Needless to say, the dogs didn't get their opossum to play with on that day. I never put my hand into another hole of any kind without first knowing what might be inside.

Grandpa always talked about eating opossum and sweet potatoes. I asked Grandma one day if she would ever cook an opossum for us. With quite a stern look, she replied, "Now, I'm not about to mess up my good pots cooking a large rat. I'm especially not about to ruin good sweet potatoes with an ol' opossum. You can have all the rabbit and squirrels you want but no opossums."

She said her family had never eaten opossums or coons. Grandma said even the thought of eating a giant rat, or anything with thumbs, made her kind of queasy.

Fishing and Sorghum

After our first year with Grandpa, summer came again, and school was out. I was sure anxious to go fishing and try out the new fishing rod and fish gig I'd got for Christmas. I asked Grandpa when we might go. He said, "If you're careful and stay at the edge of the lake, where it's backed up over the sage grass, you boys can go down to the lake tomorrow and try out your new fish gig. The water's only knee high in the grass area, but there should be some big catfish nesting in the grass."

We promised not to go anywhere else but in the grass, so early the next morning Jack and I, along with Ole Blue, walked the mile to the flooded grass area. Blue took up watch as we stalked the flooded grass area with my new fishing gig. Grandpa had attached the gig to a cane pole. After several minutes, we spotted what had to be the largest fish we had ever seen. I slipped up so close I could see the tail fin almost completely. The fish hadn't seen me, so I threw the gig as hard as possible into the fish. It struck the fish in the side, and after a large splash, I saw a five-foot-long alligator. I was so close to its head I had no trouble at all seeing its eyes and teeth, along with the knobby-looking back. I turned quickly and hollered as loud as my lungs would allow, "Run, Jack! It's not a catfish—it's an alligator!"

I am quite sure we ran on top of the water and didn't stop until we got back home. What a sight it must have been, Jack and me running at top speed, still shouting, and Ole Blue barking his head off at our heels. After we caught our breath, we managed to tell Grandpa of our close encounter with an alligator. He laughed and explained to us it was actually a fish called alligator gar. He said we would all go down to the lake tomorrow. We could look for the gig. With any luck, the gar would still be there.

The next day Grandpa, Grandma, Jack, and I went down to the lake. Ole Blue accompanied us. He seemed concerned as I walked back out into the sage grass. I looked for the gig but never found it or the gar fish. I did fish with my new rod and reel, which I'd been given last Christmas. I caught several fish. Grandma and Grandpa caught a tow sack full of catfish. Jack was even able to catch some fish. Jack, Grandpa, and Grandma all used cane poles with bobbers. Using the cane poles with bobbers seemed effortless. At times two or three poles had fish hooked at the same time.

When we got back home and were cleaning the fish, I asked Grandma, "Why were so many fish in this spot?"

She replied, "Well, the other day when you were at the lake with the ol' gar fish, your grandpa slipped down though the woods and baited the spot. He said he was watching you boys and barely made it back here before you two came running up the road. When he baits a fishing hole, he puts canned corn and chicken innards in a tow sack along with a good-size rock and throws it about ten feet out into the lake. The scent leaks into the water, but the fish can't get to it. This way they're so hungry, when our bobbers hit the water, they attack what's baited on our hooks."

The fish really tasted good at supper, and afterward I asked Grandpa where he'd learned to bait the fish. He smiled and said it was an old Indian trick. He said his people would use this method to increase their catch when netting or seining the creeks and rivers.

We caught lots of fish during the summer at Grandpa's fishing hole. It was always fun going to the lake with Grandpa and Grandma. It was never hurried, and it was hard to tell which of the four of us were having the most fun, although sometimes I think it was Grandpa. Grandma usually packed baloney sandwiches and tea. Sometimes we even had some soda pop and fried apple pies.

Grandpa also took Jack and me to a small creek that fed into Chickamauga Lake. There was a small bend in the creek, with a large mulberry tree on the edge of the creek bank. Grandpa tied a rope over a limb that hung out over the creek. Jack and I enjoyed swinging on the rope and sometimes used it to jump into the cool creek water. Grandpa never got into the creek with us but seemed quite content to watch and eat the mulberries, which were in abundance in the summers.

I still remember our first visit to this particular site. As Grandpa was attaching the rope to the tree limb, we noticed several water moccasins swimming the creek and made our fears known to Grandpa.

He replied, "They'll go away when you make enough noise. When you start throwing rocks in, they'll skedaddle."

We did as he'd said and they seemed to disappear, but I always wondered how far away they really had traveled!

One afternoon we were sitting on the bench with Grandpa. He told me to go inside and see what Grandma was fixing for supper. When I got into the kitchen, I noticed a large dish pan with a tea towel placed over it. I didn't take time to look under the towel; instead I decided to squeeze the towel and guess what was underneath. It was difficult; it didn't feel like the usual green beans, corn, or okra. I lifted the towel, and to my dismay it was a fresh cake, now torn into pieces from all my probing. Needless to say, Grandma was not pleased with my mistake. No one was able to have a very large piece of cake that night. I never checked the dishpan again without raising the towel to look inside.

This summer, like all the others, was full of the usual summer picking and canning of fruits and vegetables. When late summer came, Grandpa started gathering the press and cooking vat for making sorghum. He placed the press uphill from the cooking area. The cooking area was covered with a roof supported by poles, leaving the sides open. It made for easy access from all four sides.

We cut the cane field by hand using knives about two feet long. We loaded the cane in the horse-drawn wagon and then piled it next to the press area. It took several trips over several days to bring all the cane down from the field.

Grandpa hitched one of the mules up to a harness attached to a long pole, which turned the press. "Now I'll show you two how to feed the cane into the press. Keep feeding until I say stop. Watch your heads—the mule's going to be walking round and round pulling the pole. The mule will keep walking until I tell it to stop."

A small curved trough carried the juice from the press to the vat for cooking. A fire was kept burning under the vat day and night. A couple of neighbor men helped Grandpa with the cooking. Later, when all the sorghum had been cooked, the men were given a share.

A small tin cup was placed beside the trough next to the vat. Grandpa used it to check the sweetness of the cane juice coming into the vat. He would say, "Now, you two can always have a taste any time you want, but be careful—it can make you sick if you drink too much." We never got sick, but we were at the cup quite often. Sometimes I would catch a smile come from Grandpa as he watched us take a drink from the cup.

When Grandpa told us to feed the cane, it would take about twenty minutes or so of pressing to fill the vat with enough juice for cooking. We would take the cane stalks that had been pressed down to the hog feed area to be fed to the hogs later. Grandpa kept a watchful eye on his sorghum as it cooked. He liked it to be light to medium brown in color, with the consistency of honey. Sometimes the last of the batch would turn more black. He would say, "Scrape this out and empty it into the buckets for the hogs." He said it was called blackstrap and was not any good except for use as hog food. He also said he'd heard of people eating it, but he wasn't going to eat anything that was burnt. When I was an adult, I tried blackstrap molasses and came to the same conclusion Grandpa Will had expressed.

I enjoyed staying out by the cooking area at night. I would usually listen to Grandpa and the neighbor men talk. The conversations were about things that had happened or hunting tales. It was enchanting to listen as the fire crackled under the vat. The firelight made silhouettes of each person as he sat or stirred the vat. It's a vision I still experience, especially when I see a sorghum press.

During sorghum making, Grandma's time was spent of washing all the buckets, preparing meals for everyone, and quilting. During the days, several women would sit around a quilt frame placed under the large hickory trees in the front yard. The women seemed to enjoy visiting as they quilted. Grandma was always in view of the sorghum making and stopped quilting to bring fresh pitchers of tea to us. This always won her a big smile from Grandpa.

Timber Cutting

One summer morning after breakfast, Grandpa said, "Well, you're going to learn something about cutting timber."

He took the cross-cut saw, two axes, and several steel wedges and motioned for us to follow. As we got into the woods, he dropped the axes and wedges beside an old stump.

With a wide grin Grandpa said, "We're going to need some new boards this year, so we need to fell several trees."

He pointed to a large straight tree to our right, saying, "We'll start with this one."

Grandpa proceeded to cut a deep notch about waist high, facing downhill. He set the cross-cut saw on the opposite side of the tree as the notch, at the same height. He motioned me to get on the other end of the cross-cut saw.

"Now, only pull the saw back to you when I've finished pulling it my way, and don't ride the saw," he instructed.

It took me several tries, but finally I managed the art of sawing. As we got about half way through the tree, Grandpa stopped, leaving the saw in the tree, and drove a couple of steel wedges into the cut behind the saw.

"What's this for, Grandpa?" I asked.

"It'll help push the tree in the direction I want it to fall, which is downhill. It also keeps the saw from binding. The top of the tree needs all the limbs cut off after we fell it. It's easier to drag the limbs downhill for burning this way.

"When I say *timber,* you boys run uphill."

We sawed almost to the notch, and I started to hear a cracking noise, which seemed to get louder as every second passed.

Grandpa hollered, "Timber!" and we started running uphill. My heart was pounding in my chest as I looked over my shoulder. To my amazement, the tree had fallen exactly where Grandpa had said it would. He showed us how to trim the limbs off, leaving the ones on the bottom side. Grandpa and I then cut the tree into logs about twelve feet long. After the cuts, we removed the remaining limbs, which had been left for support.

After dinner, Grandpa harnessed up one of the mules and took him back to the woods. He'd brought along some chains with sharp spikes attached. He called the spikes *dogs*. He stopped the mule downhill from a large log and drove the dogs into the end of the log. He attached the other end of the chains to a single tree. Grandpa then led the mule to a spot down on flat ground. He removed the dogs from the log and led the mule back up to the next log.

This time after hooking up the log, Grandpa said, "Watch how smart this ol' mule is." With a loud whistle, Grandpa hollered, "Get up!" To our amazement, the mule dragged the log down next to the first log and stopped.

I thought for a minute and asked, "Why didn't we get the work team to drag the logs? They could have pulled several at one time." Grandpa smiled and said, "Why, if the team had pulled the log over a yellow jacket nest and got stung, they'd have started running and hurt themselves or someone. For sure they'd have torn up stuff with all those logs fastened behind them."

We cut enough logs to make several piles. Later that summer, a log truck came and picked up all the logs. After a couple of weeks, the truck returned with a load of fresh sawn boards and slabs, which we stacked under the barn shed. The slabs are the outside cuts of the log. They're flat on one side and rounded on the other. Since the slabs aren't much good to the lumber mill, they gave Grandpa as much as he wanted.

Grandpa and I replaced worn boards on all the buildings with the new boards. We also replaced the hog pen sides with new slabs. All the old wood we removed was taken down to the wood shed and cut and chopped into kindling.

That summer, Grandma said one morning, "Timber cutting reminds me of how I met your grandpa."

I noticed she smiled a slight smile as she spoke. I made some kind of excuse and followed her into the garden. As soon as we were out of Jack and Grandpa's hearing, I asked how they had met.

"Why, it was about my eighteenth birthday. Our home out on the mountain had burned not too much earlier that same year. My dad had met your grandpa while he'd been cutting lumber up on the mountain. Now, my daddy was the only man I ever loved more than your grandpa. He looked a lot like Abe Lincoln. He was hard-working and always spoke the truth.

"The old picture I keep on the living room wall has Will and me in it right after our twins were born.

"My dad had hired Will to help him rebuild the place. I remember Daddy saying your grandpa was the smartest young man he'd ever seen. As far as Will doing blacksmith work, Daddy said he was a natural with a forge and anvil. Daddy compared Will with a hammer on the anvil to an artist. He also said Will could look at a patch of woods and tell how many board feet of cut lumber could be produced. He cautioned me about Will's charm. He used to say Will could charm the skin right off a snake.

"Anyway, we were living down the road from the house during the rebuild. My mom was pregnant with my next-to-youngest sister. I would bring food up to the house site during the day. There were Dad, Will, and my bothers to feed. Your grandpa would sit and talk with me during dinner. My daddy kept an eye on us, but I could tell he was pleased that I was finally interested in someone he approved of. He told me Will was hesitant to work for him when Will learned who Mom was. Will had done some work for some of Mom's relatives, and they tried to underpay him. Dad said some of the family disliked Indians. I remember my mom's dad, and he was mean and quick tempered.

"Even though Dad was well pleased with our relationship, my mom was another story. She never warmed up to Will much during the summer. I thought maybe it was because of Daddy's constant praise for Will. She even said he liked Will more than his own boys. I knew better because I'd been around both Will and my dad more than Mom while they were building the new house. They both seemed to have a lot in common. Of course, Will was only about ten years younger than Dad, so they got along like brothers.

"Will was several years older than me at the time. I was barely past my eighteenth birthday. He had cut timber and been a blacksmith for the last fifteen years. He told me he started work right after the seventh grade. Your grandpa has a talent for figuring. Dad said he was quicker than anyone he'd ever seen. I loved hearing tales of Will's work adventures and especially his memories of the time spent with his father. Your grandpa said he never had time for girls before we met.

"In the fall Will asked me to marry. Even then, Mom said to do whatever I wanted, but be prepared for the ol' Indian to disappoint me. Well, I'm certainly glad I followed my heart. Your grandpa and I moved into the house my family had stayed in while the new house was being built. Anyway, that was how I met your grandpa."

Grandma's Passing

One summer Dad started enlarging the small two-room house he and Mom stayed in. He was only able to work evenings and weekends because of his work schedule. Jack, Grandpa, and I would walk up to house on the hill after supper every day. Grandpa seemed to enjoy being around the building project. He was most intrigued with the plumbing of the kitchen and bath, as this was to be the first home in Dallas Hollow to have indoor plumbing. The septic tank and leech field were a real curiosity. He seemed not to understand why all the power receptacles were needed. As summer passed, the house was completed. It had two separate bedrooms, a living room and kitchen, plus the bathroom.

Jack and I moved into the house mostly for sleeping. We ate breakfast there and caught the school bus in front of the house. After school, we would get off at our old spot and walk to Grandpa's. We performed the same chores, which had become quite familiar. When Mom and Dad arrived after work, we all ate at Grandpa's and then went to the hilltop house, where we would bathe and sleep. This schedule stayed the same for a couple more years.

One of our sisters was born the next fall, and the next was born the following fall. They stayed with Mom and Dad at the hill house, and Jack and I moved back full-time to Grandpa's.

This arrangement stayed the same for about two more seasons. Crops were planted and then harvested, followed by sorghum making and trips to the gristmill. Berry picking, canning, and apple drying times arrived. Hogs were slaughtered, and then came the salting and smokehouse operations. Hunting seasons arrived, but Grandpa seemed not as spontaneous as before. Grandma seemed to be slowing down as much as Grandpa. I could sense something wasn't right, but I couldn't be sure what it was.

Then one day Dad told Jack and me he was going to install some window air conditioner units into the hill house. I asked why, and he explained, "Now, your grandma's very sick. She's going to have surgery, and then she'll stay up at the house with your mom and me. Your aunts will take turns being with her during the day, and your mom will take over at night." He also told us we were going to keep staying at Grandpa's.

This didn't seem like such a bad thing to Jack and me, although we both were curious about how sick Grandma was. Grandpa tried to reassure us everything would be okay. He said, "She'll come through just fine. She has her faith and a strong spirit." I noticed he seemed more concerned than he was showing, but I didn't question him further.

We kept busy with the regular chores around Grandpa's. Dad and Mom would inform us of Grandma's progress after the surgery, and we usually visited her after school, before going down to Grandpa's.

About six weeks after her surgery, she told Mom she was not feeling well, and Dad drove her to see her doctor. The same afternoon Mom, Dad, and my aunts all showed up at Grandpa's. I noticed they had been crying, and I asked, "What happened?"

Dad said, "Your grandma has passed away." It didn't seem possible. She had been in such great spirits the past week.

Later I noticed Grandpa's eyes were quite red from crying. It was the first time I had seen him grieve. His voice, although strong, showed the stress of losing Grandma. Her sudden passing was obviously not something he had thought would ever happen. I knew he had lost a huge part of his life. As I grieved, I realized that now I had to be more help to Grandpa than ever. Jack and I performed all the chores, even the ones Grandpa usually did himself. This would not only be my gift to Grandpa but a tribute to Grandma Ida.

A lot of people came to Grandpa's during the week: most of Grandma's kin, our aunts and cousins, and even my grandpa's only living sister. Our uncle Carl, Grandpa's surviving twin son, had driven up from Cape

Canaveral, Florida. It was the first time Jack and I met some of the relatives. We were curious as to how most were related and where they lived.

It was my first wake. Grandpa's living room wasn't large enough, so they put Grandma's casket over at Mom's sister's place. Some of the relatives stayed at Grandpa's. People all brought food and talked of their experiences involving Grandma Ida. Some played music, while others sang along. It was almost like a church social or a family reunion.

The living room, where the casket was placed, had a piano. My cousin played at church and gave piano lessons there at the house. I had even taken lessons from my cousin, although I seemed to take after Grandpa, able to enjoy music more than play it. Several of our aunts could play, and since Grandma always liked music, the piano was rarely silent during the wake.

Smaller children played games outdoors, while the older kids talked and got to know each other better. Some we had never met. We were quite curious about what their schools were like where they lived. It was interesting to find out that while some lived far away, their lives were still very much like ours. I tried to connect each face with different sides of our families. Some looked like our grandparents, while others looked as if they were unrelated to any of the family.

I asked Grandpa why the wake was more like a party than a time of grief. He replied, "Now, we're not disrespecting your grandma. We're telling stories of the good times we had with her or singing her favorite songs.

The foods that were brought were mostly her favorites. There'll be plenty enough time to feel sad, but this night we're all here to enjoy her company one last time."

The next day the funeral home took her casket out of my aunt's house down to the church by the cemetery. Most of the family chose to walk since it was so close. Some talked and others broke out in song on the walk to the church. It was one of the only times I remember Grandpa wearing a tie and definitely the only time he was in church.

Grandpa rode across the street in the hearse with Grandma's casket to the gravesite. When he got out and stood by the grave, I saw the tears trickling down his cheeks. I'd never seen him cry before. A big part of him was lowered into the ground on that day. Grandpa was never the same after Grandma's death. Oh, he did what had to be done, but he was like a firefly without the glow. The fire had definitely been extinguished.

We stayed with Grandpa at the gravesite for some time after most of the people had departed. When we arrived back at Grandpa's place, I noticed several of my female cousins were taking quilts and other pieces from the home. As Grandpa, Jack, and I again went to the front bench, Grandpa gave a great sigh. I asked why people were taking Grandma's stuff.

Grandpa looked straight into my eyes and said, "It's okay. Those are only material things. We have her memory in our hearts. Always remember the three of us were able to be with her around the clock. She shared the tender moments with us. Those who took the items only knew her as Grandma or Ida. They might have the quilts, boys, but you two have the memories of her tucking the quilts around you on cold winter nights."

We still had our usual rabbit gum bounty during spring. We even managed to get in a few fishing trips. When planting time came around, I noticed Grandpa seemed to grow slower with each part of the process. He was still able to do the plowing, but it appeared his sparkle was starting to leave his eyes. The artistry I had always seen was never the same after that. It was like watching an artist paint without the drive for perfection. Grandpa was especially quiet in the evenings. Evenings had been so filled with Grandma's laughter. Sleeping must have been taxing. Without Grandma with him at night, he never seemed as refreshed at breakfast. By then I did a lot of the cooking, especially breakfast.

Jack and I stayed on with Grandpa, helping with the chores. Gardens were planted, and Grandma Ida's sister did most of the canning. By then the hogs had all been sold off, along with Grandpa's teams.

Within another year, my dad decided to explore the prospects for work in the Southwest. After several trips by himself, he and Mom informed us we were moving to the southern part of the state of New Mexico.

This surely sounded strange to Jack and me. We were concerned about schools, friends, new neighbors, and, most of all, leaving Grandpa.

After we were assured Grandpa would be visiting us there, we accepted the move. It took several weeks to sell unwanted items and pack for the move. Soon we were on our way.

The cross-country trip was definitely a learning experience for us all. I had read about the states we crossed, but it was not like anything I could have ever imagined. By the time we were approaching the west side of Texas, I knew it was going to be a lot different than Tennessee. The trees and grass had disappeared, along with all the familiar animals. Most of all I was already missing Grandpa.

As the temperature climbed past the hundred-degree mark, I became concerned about a place with this kind of heat, where it was important to carry water with you. Dad had acquired a canvas water bag, which he filled with water and hung over the front bumper. He said the water would slowly evaporate, causing the water to cool.

My apprehensions were calmed somewhat as we settled into the old adobe house, with its large trees and irrigation systems. Although the desert around the area reached high temperatures, our home in the valley stayed quite a few degrees cooler. I knew Grandpa would like the home whenever he came.

Grandpa's Passing

The first autumn after we moved west, Grandpa Will took his first-ever airplane trip. As promised, he had come West to visit. I sat quietly on one side of Grandpa Will, with Jack on his other side, as my father's '59 Buick Roadmaster pulled out of the El Paso Airport onto Mesilla Valley Road. I was trying to imagine what it had been like for an old Indian to fly like the hawks and eagles of his youth.

Suddenly the silence was broken. "Look at the cardboard houses, Grandpa!" Jack pointed to Shanty Town across the river in Juarez, Mexico. The late fall sun was setting behind the hills of El Paso, casting a red and orange hue over the valley. Grandpa, in his usual way, shrugged and said, "I guess they didn't have enough time or money for wood."

The ride through the pecan orchards, the irrigation ditches lined with red chiles laid out to sun dry, inspired a question from Grandpa. "Why are red and brown the only colors I see? Where are all the green trees and grass?"

We turned up the fruit-tree-lined drive to the old adobe farmhouse with its barns and corrals. The house was located in the middle of large cotton and chile fields, surrounded by large cottonwood and pecan trees.

"What's this town called?" asked Grandpa Will as he gazed out over the half-picked cotton field.

"Dona Ana. It has a post office, grocery store, gas station, and even a cotton gin," I answered. I felt proud that we'd moved to a town large enough to have its own post office.

"We don't need much wood to heat the house because it's made out of adobe, with walls two-foot thick, which also makes it easy to cool in the summer," Jack stated as we walked from the car into the house.

"It looks sturdy enough, but where's all the wood? The only wood I see is the trim around the doors and windows," returned Grandpa Will.

"You boys let Will rest for a while," said Dad as he seated Grandpa Will in front of the kiva fireplace and started a roaring fire, which quickly took the chill out of the room.

"Why is the fireplace rounded, with no rock? How can the wood burn like it's soaked in kerosene?" Grandpa Will asked, a small grin now appearing.

"It's built with a rounded front to better reflect the heat into the room, and the wood is piñon, which has a heavy sap, like turpentine," I replied.

"Where's Grandpa going to sleep?" Jack asked as he looked to Dad.

"He's going to be with you boys in the front bedroom. Why don't you show him around the house now, so your mom can get supper ready."

The next day Grandpa checked out the chickens, hogs, and calves. By now, Jack was a member of the local Future Farmers of America and was raising two calves as his class project. I could tell Grandpa missed his livestock.

We took Grandpa Will on a tour of the valley and the nearby Oregon Mountains. I was really excited because I was allowed to drive. Any chance to show Grandpa what I'd learned since our relocation West was surely a treat. When Grandpa got back home he sat in deep thought for quite some time, then he said, "You know, after we got up out of the valley it looked as if someone had washed all the dirt, trees, and grass off, leaving only rock and sand. There were no trees, berry bushes, flowering shrubs, wildflowers, or vines. I didn't see any small game, like squirrels, raccoons, opossums, or cottontail rabbits. I did see a rabbit your dad said was called a jack rabbit. It was bigger than the cottontails, but it didn't put its belly on the ground when it ate. There were no songbirds, like bluebirds, blue jays, or orioles. The frogs we saw even had horns. Your dad said there are no fireflies or katydids. The sky didn't even have clouds. Next you'll tell me there is no dew on the grass in the mornings."

Well, I knew Grandpa Will had been disappointed with his first sightseeing trip of the West. All I could think to say was, "It's sure different than the Tennessee mountains. You can see for an eternity here." I remembered what Grandpa had told me several years earlier: "I always enjoy seeing new places or meeting new people, but I don't have to like either."

He was all grins when we ate fresh tamales, Spanish rice, and refried beans for supper the same night. A neighbor had brought the tamales over. Dad had given the neighbor part of the hogs that we had butchered recently, and in return we had several dozen tamales for the coming winter.

The next week Grandpa Will watched the rest of the cotton being harvested and even visited the nearby cotton gin. He spent most of the day watching and asking questions of the gin workers. I think Grandpa would have enjoyed growing cotton in Tennessee if the boll weevils had not destroyed the cotton crops around Chattanooga during the twenties.

Grandpa seemed to enjoy picking up the pecans that had fallen from the trees that surrounded the house. Sometimes I think he ate as many as he picked. Fresh pecans were a new treat for him, as pecans weren't native to his part of Tennessee.

Soon we had a snowfall. Grandpa seemed to enjoy sitting by the Kiva fireplace and teasing my two younger sisters. Both were still too young to attend school yet, allowing Grandpa plenty of time to get to know them. Usually when he went for walks up and down the drive, the two girls would ride their tricycles alongside, which sometimes provoked a swat with his walking cane when the opportunity seemed too strong for Grandpa Will to resist.

When spring came, it brought planting time for the cotton and chiles. Watching the Mexican farm workers irrigate the fields seemed to fascinate Grandpa, but not as much as the crop duster airplane that came roaring in the first morning of dusting season. The plane came in fast and low, almost to the cotton tops. The path brought the plane parallel to the drive, which gave Grandpa a perfect view from the screened front porch. He was transfixed all morning. "Someday I want to fly like that!" I cried in excitement, but Grandpa replied, "You do, and you'll break your fool neck."

He was intrigued with how cool the house remained after the yard had been irrigated. Every time the fields received water, so did the yard.

During the summer, we took Grandpa Will around the state to as many places as possible. White Sands National Monument earned his usual kind of comment: "It's too bright to look at, and nothing grows in it."

His visit to Lincoln, New Mexico, did seem to bring a smile. I was surprised. I'd thought visiting Billie the Kid's stomping grounds would have done it. As it turned out, for Grandpa it was the story of Smokie the Bear that gave him the biggest grin. I suddenly realized the Indian in Grandpa was stronger than I had thought. I remembered that most Indians have a strong connection to the bear. I recalled the time Grandma Ida had told me of Grandpa Will and his two sisters being brought out of the Cherokee Reservation area of North Carolina to the Gatlins, who raised and gave them the Gatlin name. I wondered if Grandpa Will could remember any of his Indian youth or Indian lore. Did he have any memory of his grandfather, who would have been the correct age to remember the Trail of Tears roundup by the U.S. Cavalry? Did his grandfather hide out during the roundup, or was he part of the Oconaluftee Indians, a small group of Cherokees living off Indian land at the time and given permission to be excluded from the relocation?

We did take him to visit a couple of Indian reservations. His one comment was, "You know, I think they have it worse than my people. Why, their lands aren't nearly as good as the Oklahoma lands." I told him the northern New Mexico Indians were not relocated. He said that was probably because the government couldn't find any place worse than where they were already living.

Later that summer, Grandpa asked about fishing, and Dad told him the legendary description of the Rio Grande around our area. "It's a mile wide, a foot deep, too thin to walk on, and too thick to drink. It doesn't have fish like the Tennessee." That was all Grandpa needed to hear—if it didn't have big catfish, he wasn't interested.

He went wood cutting with us in the late summer. We loaded up the stakebed Ford truck with food, chainsaws, and axes and headed up to the Gila Wilderness area. We cut piñon and cedar into fireplace-size logs. Grandpa and I reminisced about the year he and I cut all the trees back in Dallas Hollow. At times he seemed well pleased about what we had managed to remember about falling trees. When the truck was filled with all it would hold, we stopped and ate. We made several trips there during summer. Grandpa Will agreed the chain saw was easier and more versatile for firewood cutting than the cross-cut saw.

Summer gave up two of Grandpa's favorites, peaches and watermelons. That particular summer produced above average crops of both. Grandpa couldn't keep from having a peach on almost every walk down the drive that summer. He ate his share of seedless yellow watermelons every chance he got. We managed to grow a patch of strawberries, but to Grandpa's dismay, no wild strawberries grew in the Southwest.

He seemed to also enjoy being around Jack and his FFA calves, and he told of his own past livestock raising. If Jack had horse or mule teams in the corrals, I don't know if anyone else in the family would have received any of Grandpa's attention.

As summer turned to fall, Grandpa Will was given several treats. The first was the return of the yellow crop duster airplane. Again the loud roar of the duster came fast and low.

"We have to stay inside this morning, Grandpa," I said.

Grandpa quickly replied, "But I wanted to go back out and watch." I explained that they were spraying with defoliant, too dangerous to breathe. He understood but seemed confused why it was necessary to drop the cotton leaves. When the workers with cotton-picking machines showed up a couple weeks later to strip the cotton off the plants, Grandpa seemed to better understand why the leaves needed to be removed first.

It was the time of the year when the green chile was picked and roasted. The ripe red ones were laid out on every westward-facing surface to sun dry. The air was filled with a mix of roasting green chiles and smoke from the piñon wood being burned in the fireplaces and stoves of the valley. That scent combination is still enchanting for me. The smell plus the color of yellowing cottonwood leaves and red chiles drying in the sun brings back fond memories. These are some of the things that make New Mexico the Land of Enchantment.

The other thing that fall offered Grandpa Will was ripe pumpkins. Pumpkins were the filling for his second-most-favorite pies, blackberry being first. Pumpkins were plentiful, and pie time it was. Grandpa enjoyed many slices of pie sitting close to the Kiva fireplace. He loved the crackle and smell the piñon wood gave off.

As frost settled in on the valley, Grandpa became increasingly anxious and decided it was time for him to go back to his Tennessee home. I asked if we were going to see him again in the spring. He said he wasn't sure, but he wanted Jack and me to remember our times with him. Grandpa said when his time to go back to his people finally came, I could see him by watching for eagles and hawks. He explained he would still be watching over us. When I spotted a hawk or eagle, I would see my Cherokee cheeks as I gazed skyward. This would assure me that part of him would always be with me.

In what seemed like no time after Grandpa Will left for Tennessee, Mom came outside one day and said, "I got a call from Sister Vernon—your Grandpa Will has passed away."

Jack looked over at me and said, "I never asked what his Indian name was."

I replied, "I am happy for him because he's no longer a Cherokee lost. He's with his people now, especially his grandpa. Someday when it's my time to go, I hope to meet his grandpa."

Over forty-five seasons have come and gone since the passing of Grandpa Will. Jack chose a career in the Air Force and then became a professional elk hunting guide. He now resides in Alaska, where he hunts deer, caribou, and the great bears of the north. He fishes for the wild salmon.

I worked for thirty years in the telecommunication business. I earned my private pilot wings. I flew all over the United States in my own aircraft. I was able to see eagles on several of my flights and was reminded of Grandpa Will each time. After retiring, I took up blacksmithing. Grandpa was with me each time I fired up the forge. He inspired my artistic side, if only in spirit. I toured the art circuits of the Southwest. I now reside in the Ozarks, close to the northern path of the Trail of Tears. I still love the ring of my hammer on the anvil and the ability to bring forth nature from iron.

Grandma's brother, who had lived on the old place on Lookout Mountain, passed away. When his will was read, true to his word, Grandma Ida's descendants were not given any portion of the estate. Jack and I have not felt snubbed by the results of the will. Rather, we were privileged to have shared the time with Grandpa Will and Grandma Ida. We not only received Grandpa's knowledge, but all of Grandpa's direct descendants carry his Cherokee blood lineage. The twelve years Jack and I spent with Grandpa molded us more than any other time. What we have become, I am sure, would win a large smile from Grandpa. In many ways, it would be like he was looking in a mirror. Thank you, Grandpa!

www.ingramcontent.com/pod-product-compliance
Lightning Source LLC
Chambersburg PA
CBHW020254290526
45784CB00003B/1251